Charles John Vaughan

Voices of the Prophets

Or faith, prayer, and human life

Charles John Vaughan

Voices of the Prophets
Or faith, prayer, and human life

ISBN/EAN: 9783337037260

Printed in Europe, USA, Canada, Australia, Japan

Cover: Foto ©Lupo / pixelio.de

More available books at **www.hansebooks.com**

VOICES OF THE PROPHETS

Or Faith, Prayer, and Human Life

By C. J. VAUGHAN, D.D.

VICAR OF DONCASTER

" *The voices of the prophets which are read every sabbath-day.*"—
ACTS xiii. 27

Anchora Spei

'ALEXANDER STRAHAN, PUBLISHER

56 LUDGATE HILL, LONDON

1867

₊ *This Publication completes a Series of three little Volumes, which have enabled me (through the great liberality of their Publisher) to give substantial aid to the costly work of Rebuilding my Parochial Schools.*

CONTENTS.

HUMAN LIFE.

INTRODUCTION.

A

N O picture is more familiar to us than that of the Ethiopian Nobleman returning from his worship at Jerusalem, and reading aloud, on his chariot, the Book of the Prophet Isaiah. It is a history full of instruction. It speaks of an earnestness in seeking God—a diligence in the use of light given —an exertion and self-devotion in acting upon the knowledge of duty—which is an example for all time. And it speaks too of the reward of these things : how the eye of God marks such diligence and such exertion ; how He takes care that, to him that hath, more shall be given ; how He sends instruction to the teachable, guidance to the seeker, light to the watcher ; and enables one who but now was puzzling hopelessly over the dark sayings of a Prophet, to lay hold of a directing clue and a guiding light, by which he may reach the Saviour Himself, and go on his way rejoicing.

The Evangelist Philip, guided by the express mission of the Holy Spirit, approaches the chariot of the Ethiopian stranger; hears him reading aloud, as he journeys, the Volume of inspired Prophecy; and addresses him in words as grave as they are significant, *Understandest thou what thou readest?*

Let the same question sound in our hearts this day, in reference to that completed Book, of which Philip and the Ethiopian possessed but one half, and that the more elementary and the less Evangelical half; and let it say to each one of us, not for an answer aloud, but for an answer to conscience and to the heart-searching God, When thou openest (as all Christians open) the Book of Holy Scripture, to find therein a lamp to thy feet and a light to thy path, *Understandeth thou what thou readest?*

I fear there must be, for some of us, what was needless for the devout Ethiopian, an earlier and more elementary question still, *Readest thou?*

In how many a nominally Christian home lies a Bible unread from Sunday to Sunday ! left unopened, unregarded, on the shelf or the table ! eyed (so to say) askance, as an enemy and an intruder, nor come to benefit or to comfort, come rather to torment us before the time ! Some who pray read not : how many, alas ! neither pray nor read. Consciences are sensitive upon this subject. You might bring in vain many tentative charges against a Congregation or against its members : you might draw your bow at a venture, trying one by one the arrows of remonstrance and conviction upon a sick man, dying and unawakened before you, and none should pierce and none should hit: but this, I think, might almost be depended upon, to hit at least if it pierced not, Was the Book of God your study and your meditation ? Did you daily read, daily mark it ? Was it your companion by choice, was it even your monitor by duty ? Too often day dawned and night darkened upon you—you rose and you rested—you had time for work, time for food, time for exercise, time for society—but no time for the Bible ; no time to give to the study of that record of Revelation which yet you professed to receive as your rule, to trust as your guide, to look to as your hope. Who would not have been ashamed to be seen or to be heard, like this Ethiopian, reading his Bible as he took his journey? And is that shame a good sign—a sign of a depth of reverence which cannot bear to be intruded upon, of a sincerity which dreads to be overrated? Or is it not rather a confession of neglect and ungodliness, bashful about religion in public just because it does despite to God in secret? The question, *Readest thou?* must go before the question, *Understandest thou?*

But indeed the two questions are not wholly separate and disconnected. Many read not because they understand not. They have tried many times to become interested in the Bible, and failure has made them close it. And certainly many understand not because they read not. They give themselves no chance of understanding: they do not even read.

What is it then to understand the Scriptures?

There is an understanding of the mind, and there is also an understanding of the heart.

Some parts of the Bible are difficult of explanation. There are passages in the Prophets—

passages also in the Epistles—which learned men cannot agree upon, which the uneducated cannot even guess at. Allusions to obscure events in history, to manners and customs long obsolete, to natural features now lost, or geographical arrangements now obliterated—and, on the other hand, unusual expressions or abstruse arguments such as only scholars can investigate, theologians discuss, or logicians unravel ;—these things, and others like them, make the understanding of a considerable part of Holy Scripture as difficult to the mind, as its deepest meaning must ever be inaccessible to the natural heart of man. In these respects, it may almost be said of a large portion of the Bible, as the Prophet Isaiah says of the vision of God when it came of old to His people, *It is become as the words of a book that is sealed, which men deliver to one that is learned, saying, Read this, I pray thee: and he saith, I cannot; for it is sealed: and the book is delivered to him that is not learned, saying, Read this, I pray thee: and he saith, I am not learned.*

But even where the interpretation is certain, even where the sense is plain, still it cannot be understood—nothing can be understood—without study.   It is here that men deceive themselves. They fancy that the Bible is the one book in the world which needs no labour. Most painful is it, most affronting, to Christian people, to hear men of the world fling abroad hasty, super-ficial, summary judgments upon revelation and doctrine, without so much as the pretence of having studied or reflected or pondered. *Every one knows that—Every one can judge of that—* is the language, scarcely disguised, upon God's truth and God's inspiration, on the lips of men who would think it monstrous for common sense, apart from long labour, thus to pronounce upon an art, a history, or a science. If any one is to be able to answer *Yes* to the question, *Un-derstandest thou what thou readest in the Bible?* he must at least have diligently read and earnestly studied, in all its parts, the things written therein.

And let me say—lest anything before spoken as to the difficulties of the Bible should be made into a discouragement or a stumbling-block to any— that even a poor person, even an ignorant person, even a young child, will find page after page of God's Holy Word clear and explain itself before him as he dwells upon it in patient, earnest study.

I speak now even of the understanding of it by the mind. Just as the wisest of men can know nothing of the Bible without study, so the humblest of men can know much of the Bible—even as a matter of understanding — by study. *Thou hast hid these things*, even intellectually, *from the wise and prudent, and hast revealed them unto babes.* How often, how often, do we find that true !

And how much more often, when we come to the second part of understanding, which is that of the heart ! We can all see that what the Bible speaks to in us is not the mind, only or chiefly, but the heart. A person might have read all of it many times over—read it in the Greek and read it in the Hebrew—read it with all the notes of all the commentators, and with the added help of all the travels and all the histories which could throw light upon its allusions and upon its references—and yet know nothing of it for his soul's health. The supposition is indeed unnatural : for who would care thus to know the Bible, if he cared not for a thing yet beyond—for the knowledge of it as opening to him the way of salvation ? But the two kinds of knowledge are distinct, and must be spoken of in their distinctness.

What then is it to understand with the heart?

The Ethiopian stranger did not yet understand the Scriptures, because he had not yet found in them Jesus. He was still asking, *Of whom speaketh the Prophet this*—this about the sheep led to the slaughter, and the lamb dumb before his shearer— a humiliation which deprived of justice, and a life taken by violence from the earth—*of whom speaketh the Prophet this? of himself, or of some other man?* And it was when *Philip opened his mouth, and beginning at the same Scripture preached unto him Jesus*, that he first understood, in the true sense, the thing that he read.

Even so was it with the Disciples after the Resurrection, when One greater than an Evangelist at last *opened their understanding that they might understand the Scriptures.* It was by making them see in the Law of Moses, and in the Prophets, and in the Psalms, the things concerning Himself.

Thus then no man really understands the Bible until he finds Christ in it. *The testimony of Jesus is the spirit of prophecy.* It is not only in one chapter of the Prophet Isaiah, it is all through the Old Testament Scriptures, that God is testifying of His Son. The Law testified of Him. The Moral

Law, by revealing to man his sinfulness, and making him cry out for forgiveness to One who is All-holy. The Ceremonial Law, as the Epistle to the Hebrews teaches us, by prefiguring an open way into the Divine presence through the atoning and sanctifying blood of Jesus. How much more as the revealing light cleared and brightened, till it became in the Prophetical Scriptures almost a Gospel—disclosing more and more of the work and of the glory of Him that should come, of man's utter need and of God's boundless mercy —that so there might be no lack of signs by which men (when He came) might recognize their Saviour, and no dimness or dulness of hope for those who must go to their graves before His appearing.

And perhaps we think that there can be no doubt, in Gospel times, as to our thus understanding the Scriptures. We know that they are full of Christ. The very first use made of them for us in childhood was to teach us out of them the Advent and the Ministry, the Life and the Death, of Jesus. And the chief object of our ever opening the Bible for ourselves has been this— that in some cloudy and dark day, of anxiety or of bereavement, we might find something about Him to calm our fears, and to say to the tempest of our souls, *Peace, be still!* And yet there is no doubt that the understanding of Scripture with the heart is even more rare (if it be possible) than the understanding of it with the mind. We see Christ, it may be, in the Scriptures: but do we go on to seek Him, by their help, as the Light of life, and the Anchor of the soul, and the Propitiation for personal sin, and the Source and Inspirer of an individual holiness? *Search the Scriptures, for in them ye think ye have eternal life—and they are they which testify of me—and yet, ye will not come to me that ye might have life!* Ah! it is here that we come short. We see that Christ is in the Bible: but we do not go to Him, we do not call Him in, we do not for ourselves seek nor search nor see Him there! And this last is the understanding of the heart. This last is the thing which enables a man to give an affirmative answer, when the question is put to him, apart by himself, *Understandeth thou what thou readest?*

It remains then to ask, Why not? and to ask also, How? The two questions may be combined in one brief and closing enquiry. For, if we become conscious of the reason why we understand not, we shall also be instructed at the same time how we may understand.

And here, first of all, I need not fear to say positively that, in this as in every instance, we have not because we ask not. If, not as a form, but with deep earnest truth, we always prayed the Church's Collect before we read the Bible—asking God to give us grace so to read as that we might embrace and hold fast Christ—that would be a safe and a sure step towards the understanding spoken of. How much more if we made it a matter of daily prayer that God would be pleased to open our understandings and prepare our hearts to receive Christ into them as our one Divine rest and peace and joy! But, as it is, we read the Bible, when we do read it, as if it could of itself do for us the thing which we want: as if the printed page could enter the soul, and work there by matter what is from first to last a work of spirit; as if the mere passing of the eye over the lifeless book could do by magic that office of enlightenment and salvation which the Holy Spirit of God deputes to nothing and to no one. If we would understand what we read, we must read in

God's presence what God has revealed : an earnest and solemn act of self-presentation to Him for instruction must precede every reading—and the thought, *I am here before God as His child and His disciple*, must go along with the reading—and the prayer for the implanting of what has been taught, and for its carrying out with us into life, must close the reading—or we shall have been guilty (little as we may suspect it) of forgetting God in His gifts, of dispensing with His inward teaching even while seeking and occupied in the outward.

Next to this, and scarcely second even to this in importance, I would place the consideration, that no one can love and no one can profit by the Bible, unless he is sincerely desirous to live the life which God approves. It is one practical proof—worth many laborious arguments—of the Inspiration of Holy Scripture, that sinners feel towards it just as they feel towards God. When Adam had sinned, he straightway *hid himself* (it is written) *from the presence of the Lord God among the trees of the garden.* And so, if a man is cherishing any known sin, you will always find him hiding himself from his Bible. Not only because the Bible is a religious book. He will take up a Christian biography—he will take up the narrative of a Christian's deathbed—he will take up a Volume of Sermons, and read without repugnance that which yet reproves and condemns him: he will not take up his Bible. He can more easily pray than do that. The one may be the cry of a miserable divided heart in the ear of a distant God: the other is like God coming to him, and speaking aloud in his ear the words of confutation and judgment. The man who is not sincerely desiring to make his heart clean and his life pure, will never understand—if he can help it, he will never read—his Bible. See then, on the other hand, one of the ways towards that understanding. *Cleanse your hands, ye sinners; and purify your hearts, ye double-minded.* So shall ye approach that book which has so much of God, so much of Christ, in it, not with dislike or repugnance, but with an earnest desire that ye may profit and that ye may grow thereby.

A third chief hindrance to understanding the Scriptures is the infrequency, the intermittence, of their study. We shall never understand, so long as we grudge and stint the use of them. A common average Christian thinks it his duty to read a Psalm or to read a Chapter daily. That is his maximum. Often it is cut short: often it is forgotten: often it is jostled out of his day by some call of business or pleasure, some accident of late rising or of evening drowsiness. But the rule is this. It is done, when done, as a duty; as something for the omission of which he will be punished, by doing which he will have given satisfaction to conscience and to his God. So long as this is our spirit, we may do the duty, but we shall never understand the Bible! The man who is to do this—the man who is to find Christ, to know God, by his Bible—must begin by determining to have it for his friend. *O how I love Thy word! It is my meditation all the day. His delight is in the law of the Lord: and in His law doth he meditate day and night.* You may say, that is an advanced stage of the study. It is so. But it has its beginning too. Much depends—I had almost said all depends—upon the way in which you view your Bible. Regard it as a dull book, and it will be so. Regard it as a book fit only for sickness and sorrow, and you will soon make it so. It will retire before you, sad (as it were) and reproachful, yet obedient too, into those dark and dismal chambers to which you bid it to confine itself. And then, when you would seek it there, perchance you will not find it. When you open it, it will not speak : when you call upon it, it will not answer. This is the punishment of those who in days of health have counted God's Word their enemy. But the converse is true also. Determine, God helping you, that you will love your Bible : read it, read it again—read whole books of it at one sitting, and when next you sit down with it, read them again : if anything at first puzzles you, study it, pray over it, then lay it aside, and soon study it again : that which was dark before will oftentimes be light now : what you know not now, you shall know hereafter : have the book itself always about, keep it very near you, on your desk and on your pillow : I had almost said, confine yourself to it till you can love it— and you will love it : it will begin to talk to you, it will begin to answer you, it will begin to resolve your doubts, and to stimulate your curiosity : it will accommodate itself to your mood ; it will be grave when you are grave, and it will smile when you smile : till at last you shall say with the

Psalmist, *I am as glad of Thy word as one that findeth great spoils—How sweet are Thy words unto my taste: yea, sweeter than honey to my mouth —The law of Thy mouth is dearer unto me than thousands of gold and silver!*

Then at last, when the question is put to you, *Understandest thou what thou readest?* you shall be able to answer, with a joyful heart and a good conscience, *Thou, Lord, hast given me understanding—Thou hast dealt well with Thy servant —I thank God through Jesus Christ our Lord!*

FAITH.

FAITH REPENTING.

"I have heard of Thee by the hearing of the ear: but now mine eye seeth Thee. Wherefore I abhor myself, and repent in dust and ashes."—JOB xlii. 5, 6.

FROM *faith to faith*, is St Paul's short strong way of describing the Christian life. He who has no faith is no Christian. He whose faith is anything—however weak, however wavering—is something of a Christian. He whose faith is growing—however slowly—is running the Christian race. He whose faith is perfected is already in heaven.

Now therefore, of all questions, this becomes the most critical and the most vital, Have I faith? To assist such as shall listen in answering that great question; to guide them not only to an answer, but to that answer which accompanies peace and salvation ; and then to furnish them with some directions as to the way in which they should go, that they may in due time join the spirits of just men already made perfect, in that world where faith is lost in sight—this is the threefold object of that little course upon which we now enter, when we would propose as the first of our special meditations on the great subject of Faith, the brief but pregnant thesis,

FAITH REPENTING.

We will not spend time in elaborate definitions of the two words which our subject thus brings together, Faith and Repentance. We may just call Faith a spiritual sight, and Repentance a changed mind, and pass at once to the combination which forms the point and pivot of our subject.

Faith is a spiritual sight. The seeing with the eye of the soul something which, some one whom, we cannot see with the eye of the body. Read the illustrious records of faith, as they are spread out before us in the 11th chapter of the Epistle to the Hebrews, and you will perceive that what is said of one of the heroes of faith is in substance the secret of the life and works of all the rest, *He endured as seeing Him who is Invisible.* Faith is the looking upward into the heaven above, and seeing God in Christ there ; the looking onward into the world eternal, and seeing there a life most unlike this life—a life pure and peaceful and blessed and unchanging—reserved for all who, not having seen, have yet loved Christ here, and patiently kept His word and done His Father's will, in spite of weakness and weariness and warfare and temptation, below. Faith is the looking upward, and the looking onward, above and beyond the things which are seen and temporal, and the persons who people the world that is, to the things which are unseen but eternal, and to Him whose kingdom is already open in heaven for all who, with a resolution which will take no denial, will earnestly and diligently press into it.

This is Faith. He who lives looking upward and looking onward—setting God always before him, and seeking earnestly the salvation which is in Christ Jesus—is a man of faith. It is of him that we speak in these Discourses, and say of him, first, that the man of Faith is a man also of Repentance.

Repentance, or a changed mind, has reference specially to two subjects ; sin, and God.

To repent is to regard sin differently. Once it was made light of, carelessly played with, rashly approached, indolently yielded to, or passionately fostered. Now it is seen as God sees it ; viewed seriously, judged of gravely, deeply bewailed, anxiously guarded against, avoided, dreaded, shrunk from, abhorred.

To repent is to regard God differently. Once He was trifled with, left afar off, disliked as an intruder ; His Word, His worship, His holy day disregarded ; His right as the Creator forgotten, His call as the Redeemer unlistened to and disobeyed. Now God is seen as He is ; seen as the Fountain of being, whose we are and must be ; seen as the Spring and Source of Life, whom to know is to be happy, whom to serve is perfected freedom. He who has undergone this change, this change towards sin, and this change towards God, he, and he alone, has true repentance.

Now when we speak of Faith Repenting— meaning, of course, by that expression, the man of faith repenting—we say, in effect, that Repentance itself is an act of Faith ; that Faith is necessary to Repentance, and that true Faith prompts and produces true Repentance.

It is not very uncommon, in books and sermons, to represent Repentance as going first and Faith as following. Some would even regard Repentance as perfected before Faith begins. Some would make Repentance a preliminary stage of the Christian life ; or even no stage of it—a mere preparation and clearing of the way for the Christian life ; and Faith that which comes next—beginning where Repentance ends, and wholly distinct from it and separate. And others, however unintentionally, so express themselves, as to make Repentance a sort of condition which man must satisfy in order to his coming with acceptance to receive life from God. Man must repent, and then God will forgive. No wonder that, under such teaching, Repentance has a chilling and a repulsive sound! But if the present subject—if the two words, Faith Repenting—should be fixed by God's grace in any listening ear and waiting heart, we shall both see why heretofore we have had no true repentance, and how we may obtain in the future its peaceable fruit, its abiding unchanging joy.

1. Holy Scripture is abundant in examples of

the workings, shallow or deceptive — at all
events, disappointing and fruitless—of the things
which man calls repentance. It tells of Fear
Repenting, and Vexation Repenting, and Despair
Repenting, as though to enhance and illustrate
the power of the one true heart-deep transformation, which is Faith Repenting.

(1) There was once a young man, addicted to
the sports of the field, dear to his father's indulgent
heart by reason of a certain frankness and sensi-
bility which shot now and then like a passing
gleam of sunlight over a life of selfishness and
self-indulgence, which the plain-spoken oracle of
Revelation can characterize only by the epithet
profane. And this young man had a brother,
most unlike him in natural disposition ; as calcu-
lating and purpose-like as the other was short-
sighted and impetuous : and he, taking advantage
one day of his brother's fatigue and hunger to
drive with him a hard bargain, possessed himself,
in exchange for a single meal of pottage, of those
rights of the first-born which contained in them
not only the family inheritance but the patriarchal
priesthood. Years passed away, and still the
father lived, and still the early recklessness reaped

not its full recompence of reward. At last retribution fell. He who had despised and sold his birthright, loses, years afterwards, the blessing too. Then flowed in abundance those bitter tears which are so often regarded as the infallible token, if not the very reality and essence, of repentance : but the bitter tears flowed in vain: *Esau for one morsel of meat had sold his birthright : and ye know how that afterwards, when he would have inherited the blessing, he was rejected; for he found no place of repentance, though he sought it carefully with tears.* It was the repentance of wounded pride—it was the repentance of disappointed ambition—it was the repentance of natural resentment : it was not the repentance of grace—it was not Faith Repenting.

How often have we mourned over the late-discovered consequences of some youthful folly or more mature transgression ; bitterly accusing ourselves of an act of which all the sweetness has vanished, but of which the sting, it seems, must be perpetual till life is ended ! How have we lashed ourselves for the folly, till we persuaded ourselves that we were even penitent for the sin ! And yet how wide the difference between regret and repentance! How anxious the question for each one of us, which of the two is ours! Is our sorrow from God and toward God? or is it but that *sorrow of the world* of which an Apostle has written that it even *worketh death?* It is Faith only, it is not vexation, which repents.

(2) Centuries passed away, and the younger brother's house has grown into a nation upon the earth. For four hundred years that nation has been growing and multiplying under a pressure of servitude and of severity which might have been expected to be its extinction. At length God, the God of its fathers, has come down to see its sorrows. By a long and awful series of miraculous judgments, He is making the oppressor willing to let Israel go free. But again and again, just when the end seems to be gained, the tyrant king relapses into his obduracy. *Entreat the Lord for me,* he said again and again in the hour of his humiliation, *and I will let the people go.* But as soon as he *saw that there was respite, he hardened his heart. I have sinned this time: the Lord is righteous, and I and my people are wicked. Entreat the Lord (for it is enough) that there be no more mighty thunderings and hail: and I will let you go, and ye shall stay no longer.* The great leader

listened ; he *went out of the city, and spread abroad his hands unto the Lord: the thunders and hail ceased, and the rain was not poured upon the earth.* But when the king *saw that the rain and the hail and the thunder were ceased, he sinned yet more, and hardened his heart, neither would he let the children of Israel go.* It was the repentance of fear—it was not Faith Repenting.

O, what a Book is God's Word for unravelling the mazes of the heart of man ! Which of us has not in some moment of fear registered against himself in heaven some vow of repentance soon to be forgotten ! Who shall count the promises made on deathbeds? Who shall discriminate, save One alone, the reality and the unreality of the repentances of battle-fields and shipwrecks? Leave not we such a work for such a moment ! Ours be the repentance of a calm but earnest faith ; not the repentance of a sudden terror, of *a fearful looking for of judgment !*

(3) These are two examples of a Repentance not of faith and therefore not effectual. Take yet a third, from a time yet more eventful and a scene more sacred still.

It was the time when the Son of God stood in

human form upon the earth; when He was speaking God's words and doing God's works and fulfilling perfectly the will of God below.   There was one amongst His own chosen followers, who lived with Him without loving Him.   By degrees the breach widened and deepened, until a deliberate act of treachery sacrificed the Master's life.   We might have thought that one who could plan and execute such a crime, must have been hardened beyond the possibility of penitence.   But it was not so.   *Judas, which had betrayed Him,* St Matthew writes, *when he saw that He was condemned, repented himself, and brought back* the price of the betrayal *to the chief priests and elders, saying, I have sinned in that I have betrayed the innocent blood.*   Conscience awoke yet once more, even in him, and wrought there something to which Holy Scripture does not altogether refuse the nominal title of repentance. But that repentance was not of faith, and therefore, when it was finished, it brought forth not life but death.   The repentance of remorse and despair ended not in amendment but in suicide.   Before, or almost before, his Master was in Paradise, Judas had ended by his own hand the life which had betrayed His.   *He departed, and went and hanged himself.*

And O, how many a repentance, since that day, has produced the same deadly fruit! Sin seen, too late, to be exceeding sinful—sin seen without Christ—seen in its true character, and seen in its real consequences, but seen apart from that *blood of sprinkling* which alone can make the sight endurable—has not only rendered life miserable, it has driven the sinner on to that act of self-destruction which is the seal and signature of his ruin. The repentance of disappointment, the repentance of fear, may be shallow or short-lived ; the repentance of remorse, the repentance of despair, may even close recklessly upon the sinner the door of grace for ever. God in His great mercy keep us all from that end!

2. The same Word of truth, which shows us, by doctrine and example what Repentance is not, teaches us also what it is : sets before us Faith repenting : exemplifies to us the working of that grace which is man's life, in this particular department, its relation to personal sin and to our recovery and restoration from it.

It is altogether deceptive and mischievous language to represent sin as finally done with so soon as a man comes to Christ for salvation.

Past sin is not then done with, and present sin is not then done with.   The Christian life has to take account still of both.   And then for the first time can that account be taken rightly, when a man knows in whom he believes, and is able to commit to Him with confidence the keeping of his eternal interests.   It was when the Patriarch whose words are before us could say for the first time to his God, *Now mine eye seeth Thee,* that all his self-confidence and self-esteem gave way at once, and he can add, from the depths of a contrite soul, *Wherefore I abhor myself, and repent in dust and ashes.*   It was the thought of his sin as sin against God his God which made David utter the words of the 51st Psalm : it was the look of Jesus which broke Peter's heart, destroyed for ever his forwardness and self-parade, and made him go forth to weep bitterly, and come back converted to strengthen his brethren.

The two great lessons of our subject are these.

(1) *Only faith can repent.*   If you would be a penitent man, you must be a man of faith.   So long as you pore over the records written within of past transgression and vileness, hoping to reach repentance by means of a truer estimate and a

livelier consciousness of your own demerit and
sinfulness, not only will you never know peace,
you will never feel as you ought your own guilt.
Begin, rather, at the other end. Begin by falling
at the feet of Jesus. Begin by laying hold upon
the one hope set before you in the Gospel ; the
hope of a free forgiveness, of a perfect absolution,
through the one all-perfect all-sufficient sacrifice
made by Him for all sin. See your own sins as a
re-crucifixion of the Crucified. See Him, nevertheless, bearing them on the Cross for you, that
you might go free. Lay hold upon the Atonement
there made ; upon the love which laid all upon
Christ ; upon the love which took upon itself all
the load ; upon the love, unexhausted and untir-
ing, which still says to you, after all these years of
provocation and backsliding, *Come unto me, and
I will give you rest—My grace is sufficient for thee—
The blood of Jesus Christ His Son cleanseth us from
all sin.* By degrees, in the daily study, in the
hourly use, of that glorious revelation, the forgiveness of sin, of all sin, for the alone merits of our
Lord and Saviour Jesus Christ, there will rise up
within you, as never otherwise, as never before, a
sense of the evil of sin, and of your own deep

defilement with it, such as will find its best expression in the memorable words, *I have heard of Thee by the hearing of the ear, but now mine eye seeth Thee: wherefore I abhor myself, and repent in dust and ashes.* Faith only can repent.

(2) *Faith must repent.* It is a sad thought, to any one who is in the least degree taught of God, how slightly Christian people deal with their own sins; how they dismiss from memory and conscience past years of negligence and ungodliness; how they make it almost a duty to *forget the things behind*—not in St Paul's sense, as the repudiation of self-complacency and over-boldness, but in a sense most opposite, as the dismissal, from concern and remembrance, of all that is disheartening and saddening in the years that are gone. Not so did St Paul. It is evident that he retained to the end of his course a deep and even anxious recollection of the long period of his unbelief. *Less than the least of all saints—The least of the Apostles, not meet to be called an Apostle—Once a blasphemer, a persecutor, and injurious—Sinners, of whom I am chief*—such are the honest earnest words which express his opinion of himself, in reference to the time when he was a stranger to

Christ, and to its abiding influence upon his Christian standing. A man of faith is kept humble to the end by the memory of the sins of his youth.

But is it only in reference to the long past, to the far-distant sinfulness, that he is thus penitent still? How does each day, as it runs its course, give room and reason for the exercise of a new repentance! Good left undone, and evil done, day by day—bad habits but half broken, and better habits but half learned—opportunities of receiving spiritual benefit, and opportunities of influencing others towards godliness, every day neglected, set aside, or sinned away—yes, to the very end the Repentance of Faith must be *new every morning*, and the aspect and attitude of the believing be also to the last hour of life the aspect and attitude of the penitent.

Let us earnestly foster in ourselves this grace, which is the grace of saints. Even faith may become over-confident, may fall back little by little into a self-reliance and a levity and a presumption most unbelieving, most unchristian, most displeasing to God. Let it not be so with us. Let us sink low that we may rise high. Let us *humble ourselves* day by day *under the mighty hand of God, that He,* not we, *may exalt*—and that, not all at once, but only *in due time.* Such self-abasement will be the measure of our growth in grace and in the knowledge of Jesus Christ. *I have heard of Thee* long and often *by the hearing of the ear; but now mine eye seeth Thee: wherefore I abhor myself, and repent in dust and ashes.*

FAITH RESOLVING.

"The God of heaven, He will prosper us: therefore we His servants will arise and build."—NEH. ii. 20.

THE Repentance of Faith—our first subject—leads on to the Resolution of Faith, which is the second. *Faith Repenting:* and now, *Faith Resolving.*

No doubt the first subject might have been made to include the second. Resolution may be viewed either as a fruit or as a part of Repentance. For the sake of clearness we have distinguished the two.

In each case the point lies in the combination of the two words which form the thesis. There is a repentance which is not of Faith, and certainly there are resolutions which are not of Faith. We desire to enter into judgment with our own souls, in reference to our standing in the Christian life ; which is, from its first step to its latest, a life of Faith. We desire to see whether our repentances —for all men have something so called—are real or counterfeit repentances ; whether, when they come to us, they come out of fear, out of disappointment, out of punishment, out of remorse ; or whether they spring out of that true and living faith, which is the sight of things unseen, the sight of Him who is invisible. And we desire to see whether our resolutions—for all men know what it is to form resolutions—spring out of that faith which is the conviction of spiritual realities, the apprehension of a living and Almighty Person, or out of something else, which may indeed prompt resolutions, but not the resolutions of a Christian, not the resolutions which accompany salvation. We desire to know this, that, while there is time, we may refuse the wrong kind and choose the right. We would put away the first, that we may establish the second.

There is a strong tendency in all human teaching to be one-sided. The truth of God, like the city of God, *lieth foursquare:* but men are evermore altering that perfect shape, and making it, instead, all length or all breadth; all lines or curves or angles, instead of that full and fair proportion which God the heavenly Architect has assigned to His work.

In nothing is this tendency shown more strongly than in that which is our subject now: the subject of Resolution; which may be briefly defined as a determination of the Will for action.

It is the first idea in most minds, that they have only to will and they can of course do. It is an idea implanted in us by nature; an idea inherent in that of duty, of responsibility, of judgment; an idea which the Fall has not destroyed, and which the Gospel itself recognizes even while it corrects. Free will is the condition of action; the birthright of the moral being; the starting-point of effort, and the keystone of accountability. In any scheme of morals, in any system of religion, in any voice of revelation, there must be place found for the human will, there must be the assertion of its existence and (in a certain sense) of its independence, if there is to be either an echo from the conscience or a strength for the life. If you cannot say to a man, *This is the way—then walk in it;* if you cannot appeal to him as one who has

the power to refuse the evil and choose the good ;
if you cannot *reason with him of righteousness and
temperance and judgment to come,* as things which it
is a matter of duty to seek, to practise, and to
prepare for ; you make the world one vast mad-
house, in which the chain and the padlock must
take the place of liberty and self-management, because reason has left her throne, and force only can
prevent mischief or secure decency.   The will of
man may be enfeebled, biassed, besotted, even en-
thralled ; the man himself may rust it by indolence,
blunt it by misuse, spoil it by folly, begrime it by
vice : but even in that man it exists still, and
each step of its deterioration has been (strange as
may be the paradox) not taken by another but
taken by itself.   It was the act of the will which
in each instance weakened and damaged the will :
and when it lies at last, a helpless, corrupt, and
reprobate thing, it lies so by its own choice, and
the ruin which is its curse was its own working
too.

There is in all men this consciousness.   Even
those who complain the most loudly of the thral-
dom of their will to evil, are the most keenly sensitive to its possession and to its misuse.   They

know that they have a will, and that by their own will they have lost its force.

Language may easily be used in the name of the Gospel—fortified even by Gospel texts—which yet is not true nor wholesome language. I do not doubt that habits of sin have been fastened upon some men by telling them that they were power-less to resist. The food of the healthy is the poison of the sick. Words which to a Christian man express only his own conscious unworthiness —his inability to stand before God in his own strength, or to earn for himself by merit the re-compense of the great reward—may be to a care-less half-awakened soul a very lullaby of indiffer-ence, neutralizing the strivings of conscience, and at last paralyzing the energies of action. It is time enough to speak of moral impotence, when we see pride and self-confidence dominant : to the ear of apathy and self-complacency the proper call is that which reminds of duty, and declares that that which God commands, His creature must rouse himself to perform.

Unwholesome doctrine, on this topic of ac-countability and free will, has much to answer for, in reference to the careless lives and evil habits

of members of Christian Congregations. Education has a solemn office in sounding into the
ears of children the lesson of strict duty and inevitable retribution. The discipline of a Christian
home and a Christian school rests entirely for its
justification upon the reality of the free will. Do
this—you can do it—and you shall have praise for
the same. Do not this—you can avoid it—and
you shall suffer. Form this habit—you can—of
thought or speech—and it will bring you reward
—you will have done well. Form this other, this
opposite habit—but you need not—and it will
be your trouble, your foe, your perpetual punishment. It is thus—not by the repetition of the
words, but by the daily enforcement of them in a
discipline not all joyous but often for the present
grievous—that the child of impulse and indolence
grows by degrees into the man of activity and
self-control; into a condition the very opposite of
that which would have been reached by perpetual
allowances for human frailty, or incessant inculca-
tions of the doctrine of human impotency.

And the more the young man or the old man
deals on this principle with himself; saying, in
regard to each question that comes before him of

doing or not doing, *This ought to be done, therefore it can be done—This ought to be resisted, this thought, this word, this action, therefore it can be, and therefore it shall be*—the happier and the truer and the godlier will life itself be : much trouble will be saved, much misery escaped, much evil-doing prevented: Angels and good men will have more to rejoice in, and the enemies of God Himself will find the less cause to blaspheme.

Man, even fallen man, has a will, and God requires him to exercise it.

The man who cannot resolve is but half a man.

And yet there have been those who have so stated this principle, as to make it false in fact and subversive of the Gospel.

Some men say, What more do I want? I have a will: I know what is right: I have only to resolve, and I can do all things. Living thus, what has God Himself to say against me?

We see at once, when the thought is breathed in words, how dreadful it is. More unpleasing in the sight of man, more offensive to the eye of God, than any prodigal or any Publican, is that cold self-satisfied Pharisee, who sees in himself no flaw, sees consequently in the Saviour of sinners *no beauty that he should desire Him.*

This man has evidently not apprehended the whole of the truth, when he seized that one fragment of it, the freedom of the will.

And to confine ourselves strictly to the present subject, he has evidently caught but one of the two words before us—*Resolving,* but not *Faith Resolving*—and he shows us, in a living instance, how needful is the conjunction and the combination. There is a Resolution which is not Christian: there is a Resolution which is not of Faith.

Free will is one element of truth: free grace is the other.

The God of heaven, He will prosper us: therefore we His servants will arise and build. Or, in corresponding words less figurative, *Work out your own salvation with fear and trembling: for it is God that worketh in you both to will and to do of His good pleasure.* The resolutions of Nature are weak, shallow, and partial: the resolutions of Faith, like the inspirations of their Author, are thorough, heart-deep, life-wide, and effectual.

Look at each. Ponder, then contrast them.

1. *Nature resolves.*

Resolves, perhaps, to get rid of a fault.

We will not ask how the fault got there; nor
stay to remark that there must be something in-
complete in Nature, something defective (in other
words) in the condition of the free will, to have
allowed a bad habit to establish itself in a being
which ought to have been upright. We will take
it up where it is. There is something wrong.
Wrong, perhaps, in a child: a little trifling trick
of ill-temper, untruthfulness, or disobedience.
Wrong perhaps in a boy: those which have been
mentioned in the child, and, added to them, something a little worse—I need not say of what kind—
selfishness, cruelty, or sensuality. Wrong in a young
man : by this time, worse things still—beginnings
of self-indulgence, intemperance, or sinful lust. It
matters not, in this respect, either the age of the
person, or the kind of thing. For in this point—
the resolutions of Nature—all ages and all sins are
alike. The fault, or the sin, has become trouble-
some. I thought I was master. I thought I could
say at any moment to my own sin, Thus far shalt
thou come and no further. But I was mistaken.
I fall when I would stand. I seek it yet again,
when I would abstain. Even when I would do

good, the evil is present with me. Then I must seriously appeal to the strong will within. I must rouse my dormant energies, I must rally my scattered troops, I must turn out this intruder, I must reign again undisturbed in the citadel of my own being. *Nature resolves.*

Ah! who has not heard the saying, *Hell is paved with good resolutions?* Who that has ever fallen into a bad habit has not found in himself the justification of that sad proverb? In childhood, in boyhood, in youth, in age, we sin and resolve—resolve and sin again; sometimes, it may be, because the resolution is weak—because it does not rise to the emergency—because there is a lingering longing half-reserve all the time within, favouring the foe whose expulsion is the enterprise; but sometimes in spite of the utmost force and concentration of purpose—in spite of an experience of misery bitterly learned, and an intention of amendment as vehement as it was sincere. Such is the record, tear-blotted and blood-stained, of ten thousand times ten thousand human lives; lives oscillating perpetually between wickedness and virtue, because the power of habit was too strong for the resolution of nature, and the soul that was just *escaping as a bird out of the snare of the fowler* was again and again, in spite of itself, *entangled therein and overcome.*

But it might be said, these are exceptional cases. Here the strength of the will has been lost by evil habit. No wonder the blunted instrument cannot all at once recover the edge of its blade and the strength of its wielding, and cut down that evil growth which it has once and for long acquiesced in. Nature could have resolved, if now she cannot.

Let us take then another case.

Nature resolves to live a life of virtue.

This was the actual endeavour of one man who has—and doubtless of many who have not—left a full account of it.

For a time all seemed to prosper. The life was moral; the religious aspect of it outwardly perfect: there was even a high estimate of duty, and a great zeal for God.

The man thought himself perfect.

At length the Law of God (as he expresses it) *came* to him. Came home, I suppose, as a real thing: not as a mere written book, but as a voice of authority, as a word of command. It

came into the deep places of conscience, and said,
Thou shalt not so much as desire that which is
forbidden.   It reached forth into the distant parts
of the life, and said, God is everywhere : no province of the being is without His domain : everywhere and in all things thou must walk as in His
presence.

Then was kindled a flame of rebellion in the
moral being. Desire forbidden was even stimulated
by the prohibition.   Sin, dead within, revived as
under the ray of a tropical sun forcing matter into
vitality.   The *fair show in the flesh* was turned into
rottenness, and the supposed perfection of duty
was found to be a mere enmity and hatred against
God.

At last there came into the world One bringing
a true message from the living God in heaven : a
Man who would make religion real, and who could
not be induced to accept conventional phrases or
ceremonial observances in the place of a soul's
homage and a life's devotion.   And when He was
found to be resolute, and men could not either
intimidate or use Him, they seized Him at length
in the holy city, and, calling in for once the hated
foreigner, crucified Him by Gentile hands, and

thought Him vanquished—when, lo! out of this death there sprang an invincible life, and disciples of the despised Nazarene became the one influence upon earth. And all men must take their side, in regard to this new Religion—he whom we have described among them—the man whose resolution for virtue had thrown him into insurrection against God: and he, of course, went against the Nazarene—*persecuted* His followers *even unto strange cities, and when they were put to death gave his voice against them !*

The resolution of Nature was a resolution against Grace.

All this may sound visionary or obsolete in some ears: but let a man take it home—let him express it in modern language and apply it to present circumstances—and it will become real enough, and alas! true enough in relation to the world of this century and a Church calling itself Christian.

Many have resolved in our days—and it is a noble resolution, as it was in Saul of Tarsus—to be men of high attainment in virtue. The resolution was formed early enough to prevent a youth of vice: they estimated the life to which they

D

aspired, and it contained in it at least three in-gredients—personal, domestic, and social purity.

In the pursuit of this perfection they trusted to the firmness of the resolution, to the strength of the will. God entered not into it—save as the God of creation and perhaps of judgment—the Framer of the moral constitution, and possibly the Arbiter of the individual destiny. Him they acknowledged, probably, in the decent mainten-ance of religious forms: but they sought Him not as necessary to the acquisition of that virtue which they had proposed to themselves as the goal of their race.

Now I will not doubt that the life corresponded to this beginning. That, in the case supposed, the end aimed at was reached. The life was blame-less, exemplary, useful. The conscience remained unsullied : the home was peaceful, and the career honourable.

But I will venture to say that, even in this most favourable case, the resolution of Nature had at least three fatal defects.

First, there was no real concord and conscious communion between the soul and its God.

Secondly, there was no deep and all-sufficient consolation under the inevitable trials and eventual separations of a life of change and a death of pain.

Thirdly, there was no room here for Christ. He was not wanted as the Propitiation for sin. He was not admitted as the humbler of human self-sufficiency, or the alone strength of human weakness. To the best resolution of nature Christ can only be what He was to Saul of Tarsus in the days of flesh and the Law; a superfluity, an offence, a stumbling-block, and a foolishness.

2. *Faith resolves.*

That is, the man of faith resolves; and resolves as a man of faith—in the exercise of his faith. *I will go forth in the strength of the Lord God. The God of heaven, He will prosper us: therefore we His servants will arise and build.*

The Christian life is one of perpetual resolutions.

(1) Conscience, or the Bible—the conversation of a friend, or the ministry of the Word—has suggested to me some grace in which I am defective, or reminded me of some fault to which I am prone. The first step is Repentance: the second step is Resolution. The general has become the particular. The power of faith has to

be turned in a particular direction. The engine
of grace must be brought to bear upon a particular
part of the building. It may be that Prayer has
been too brief or too superficial. It may be that
I have thought too little of the Congregation; of
its prayer, its preaching, or its Sacraments. It
may be that my conversation has been marked by
symptoms of levity, of vanity, of censoriousness.
It may be that some root of bitterness has revived
within; some old sin, once apparently conquered,
has again raised its head, and if I would escape
utter defeat, discomfiture, and ruin, I must crush,
I must tread it down, I must eradicate it. The
first step is Repentance: the second step is Resolution.

But what resolution? A resolution of Faith.
And what is that?

First, an earnest calling in of Him in whom
I believe. This is the very name given in Scripture to Christian people. *They that call upon the
Lord. Those who call habitually upon the name of
the Lord.* They who in everything call upon and
call in Jesus Christ. This which the resolution
of Nature wholly omits, is the first and foremost
element of the resolution of Faith.

And then, not a mere idle waiting for Jesus Christ
to do all for us, without thought, care, or toil of
ours. An earnest calling in of Christ, and then
an earnest going forth in His strength to do the
neglected good, or to cast out the sin har-
boured.

And once more, not merely a calling in, and
a going forth, but a posture and attitude (as
it were) of dependence and of expectation, suitable to one who has a serious undertaking on
hand, for which he wants, and must have, all the
help and all the grace which is in the Omnipotent
and the All-holy.

These are the special resolutions of Faith,
answering to the special resolutions (above dwelt
upon) of Nature.

(2) But there is also, as before, a general resolution, bearing upon the life as a whole : an ideal
proposed, and a goal made for.

The man of faith says to himself, This and this
must I be in life, and this and this in death. To
me to live must be Christ, and to me to die must
be gain. How can this be? Every energy must
be knit up for this great enterprise; the greatest
enterprise, by far, which can be presented to a

responsible immortal being.   Before I die, I must
be this.   If so, I must be this while I live; lest,
coming suddenly, Christ find me something else—
something which cannot be with Him because it is
not like Him.   Then I must begin now—begin this
day.   I must study my great Example, to see what
I ought to be.   I must commune with Him who
is my Life, that I may grow by degrees into His
likeness.   Every day that I live, I must take a
step onwards.   It is a perpetual race.   Each day
is an epitome of life : each night is a rehearsal of
death.   In proportion as I give myself to the
work, I shall be interested, engrossed, absorbed
in it.   In proportion as I get nearer to Christ,
who is my Life and my Resurrection, I shall be
nearer to holiness, to happiness, to my home.
Not in my strength, but in His—not by looking
inward, but by looking upward—upward to the
throne of God, and to Him that sitteth thereon—I
will press to my mark.   *From faith to faith—*
faith repenting, faith resolving—faith working, faith
resting—faith militant, faith at last triumphant—
such be my life, and such my end !   *The God of*
heaven, He will prosper me: therefore I His ser-
vant will arise and build.

III

FAITH WORKING.

"Let me now go to the field, and glean ears of corn after him in whose sight I shall find grace."—RUTH ii. 2.

REMEMBERING *without ceasing your work of faith.* The Repentance of Faith, and the Resolution of Faith, is followed in due order by the Work of Faith. That is no true Repentance which does not resolve : and that is no true Resolution which does not work.

WORK.

Work has many aspects. It may be treated as a portion of man's curse.

In the sweat of thy face thou shalt eat bread, was one section of the original curse.

But it was not work which was new to man.

From the beginning work had been assigned to him : the difference was that work henceforth was to be both excessive in degree and comparatively unremunerative. The earth was to bring forth in great part thorns and thistles in return for labour: and that labour was to be no longer moderate and wholesome, but wearisome and disproportionate.

Still for fallen man work was also a safeguard. It is in the idle heart, it is in the indolent life, that the rankest weeds of evil grow : a toil so hard as to be the gradual undermining of the physical strength, is yet the protection of the moral and may be the safety of the spiritual being.

And not only so. Let the labouring man compare lives with the luxurious, and his lot will be found on the whole to be the happier. *The sleep of a labouring man is sweet*, says the Book of Ecclesiastes, *whether he eat little or much : but the abundance of the rich will not suffer him to sleep.* If work is not always happiness, certainly idleness is always misery.

And yet once more : there is a dignity too in work. God Himself works : works all days alike : works, as none else, without intermission and without repose. Else would the universe be broken up, order become again chaos, and life death. If Christ can say, *My Father worketh hitherto, and I work,* such a sentence elevates at once the humblest toil, dignifies the meanest, and consecrates the commonest.

Now since work is thus universally God's ordinance for His creatures ; even for His holy Angels who have never fallen ; an ordinance on the whole beneficent, and destined (we trust) to be perpetuated even in that *new heaven and new earth wherein dwelleth righteousness ;* an ordinance in the keeping whereof He Himself goes before, and calls upon man to be but His follower and imitator ; it is plain that the religion of our Lord Jesus Christ could not leave this great topic untouched ; could not possibly fail to say something about work ; about its place in the system of the Divine life in man ; about its proper motive and method, about its duty, its blessing, and its reward.

The Gospel of Christ does *not* leave work out. On the contrary, it is full of it. And when we take now for our subject the brief but comprehensive thesis, Faith Working, we know not how to grasp or to handle it ; so wide is its reach, so large its compass, so manifold its application.

Men have quarrelled oftentimes about Faith and Work. They have tried to set the one against the other, and asked which of the two it is which justifies. We shall not enter into that vexed question. We shall only say very briefly, that, where one of the two is certainly, there, as of course, is the other really. Faith which works not, is not, in God's sense, faith : and work which springs not of faith is not, in God's sense, work.

The two words, Faith Working, seem to remind us that there are other things which work besides Faith. Let us set before our minds, first of all, two or three of these other labourers in the great work-field of life, that we may see afterwards how they differ from their one Christian and Evangelical rival, which is the grace of Faith.

1. *Nature works.*

Sometimes in the mere consciousness of health and vitality. There is that in a man which will not and cannot be idle. If his position is such that he wants nothing ; that he *has all and abounds* by no exertion of his own ; wealth left to him from his forefathers, a home furnished and a

table supplied from day to day by dependents
whom he feels not the cost of lodging and
feeding and paying for their service ; then, rather
than endure the wretchedness of utter inaction,
he will make a toil even of his pleasures : he
will *rise up early and late take rest*, spend wearisome days for the *sake* of toil, that he may even
deceive himself into the thought that he is busy,
and escape that tedium of indolence against which
he bears witness half unconsciously that it is the
very foe of peace. Thus even Wealth works.
The Esaus of a luxurious home will take their
quiver and their bow, and go to the field day by
day to hunt for their venison.

And certainly the opposite of wealth works.
Want works. A large part of the human family
literally eats its bread in the sweat of its face.
For how many millions of homes, at this moment,
is the father of the family the winner of its bread,
and the mother of the family the patient, uncom-
plaining, yet (to speak plainly) drudging house-
wife ! Want works : works that it may live : works
that it may supply life to those whom God has
given to it as its own.

And does not Covetousness work—and Avarice work—that *love of money* (in some one or other of its forms) of which an Apostle writes that it *is a root of all evil?* When want is satisfied, wishing begins. The lust of having is not filled with getting : and to add this grain and that to an already heaped up store, is found as powerful an incentive to labour as that first urgency of necessity which made the man ask, *What shall I eat, and wherewith shall I be clothed?* Where is he who really knows when he has enough, or counts that a reason for repose, which he can possibly turn into a motive for labour?

And does not Ambition work? Men, on the one hand, who want nothing—men, on the other hand, who desire nothing—of the vulgar wealth of this world, will yet spend ceaseless toil upon the pursuit of honour. What is it which makes men politicians—whether in the small affairs of a town, or in the great interests of a nation? What is it which makes men willing to spend in a sultry arid city weeks and months of a glorious summer, which is enriching their distant fields and gardens with a beauty lost upon their possessor? Ambition—in one of its forms or in

many—the ambition of fame, or the ambition of
power, or the ambition of fashion, or the ambition
of importance—this reconciles a man to anything :
Ambition works : works with an earnestness and
a devotion which it is hard sometimes to distin-
guish from self-sacrifice.

And does not Knowledge work—knowledge,
and the thirst of knowledge? What is to come,
in ten thousand cases, of all this accumulation of
wisdom? For one man who rises to distinction by
writing, thousands live laborious days and nights
in reading : this appetite, like others, grows by
indulgence ; and every year sends to the grave
many a mind filled with undivulged secrets of
knowledge, and many a brain prematurely worn
out by relentless and now profitless researches.
Work has its victims as well as its votaries : and
no insignificant portion of these are men who have
martyred themselves in knowing.

Do we blame indiscriminately these workers who
are not yet of Faith? Doubtless human life is the
gainer by every kind and department of industry.
The labourers of society are its benefactors. Better
any work than any idleness.

And we must add yet one more to the list of workers; one which comes nearer than any before it to that of which we are in quest, and yet stops short of being that which alone is distinctively Christian.

Duty works.   There are those who are brought day by day to the performance of the task set them, not by inclination, but in spite of it; not from a superabundance of energy which must have its vent, but rather with a conscious lack of energy which must be made up for by the mere sense of duty.   There are men who would give much for repose : men, too, who might rest without wanting : men, too, for whom the world has found no honour—whose business is uncongenial to them if not repulsive, and who ply it from youth to age without expectation of success or hope of change.   And yet they work.   Duty works, as well as want, or covetousness, or ambition, or the thirst of knowledge : Duty works also ; works on principle ; and seems at first sight to miss scarcely by a hair's breadth that higher, that highest attainment, the working of a principle which is not of this world, the spiritual gift and grace of faith.

2. *Faith works.*

And a very little consideration will show us some definite points in which the work of Faith differs from any of those industries of which we have hitherto spoken. The little Parable of the text will then be expounded, and we shall hear Faith saying, in reference to the life-work proposed to her, *Let me now go to the field, and glean ears of corn after Him in whose sight I have found grace.*

(1) *The work of Faith looks within.*

Nothing can be plainer, and yet nothing is more often forgotten, than that out of the heart (in all senses) are the issues of life. *Out of the abundance of the heart the mouth speaketh.* Speech, Christ says, is the mere overflow of the heart. And so action is nothing but the expression of an inward principle; the coming out of something which first is within. These things, to a Christian, are self-evident. But when we go on to apply them, some dispute, some mistake, almost all evade them.

Life, we say, is seen by God in its spring. It is not the performance, by daily routine, of a certain number, nor even a certain kind, of separate acts. It is not the mere discharge of the offices

which belong to the particular station in which
God has placed us. It is not merely a careful
attention to business, a studious regard to propriety, nor even the addition to these of a regular
and decent attendance upon the ordinances of
Divine worship. There is nothing, in any of these
things, or in all of them, which necessarily implies
there being anything left when this mortal husk
and shell is stripped off from the soul which it
encases. All these things may have been done
and well done, and yet the immortal soul, when
it has shuffled off its bodily circumstance, may
find itself utterly unqualified (to say the least) for
that standing before God, and still more for that
dwelling with God, which is the thing which comes
after death, the thing which is to be through
eternity. The question, *What will you do in
heaven?* is one which may well sound with dis-
quietude and consternation in many ears not of
the profane or dissolute, not of the blasphemers of
God or of the open injurers of man.

The work of Faith then, unlike other works,
begins within. Faith, which is the sight of the
unseen, apprehends the existence of spirit, the possibility of regeneration, and the direct influence of

Divine grace upon the heart and soul of man. It would not be faith—in the Christian sense—if it did not apprehend these mysteries. Before Faith can set out upon her gleaning, she must find grace in the sight of One unseen. One half of her work, and that the primary and the most essential, has to be done within. Not indeed that the outward work can stand still until the inward work is accomplished. Day by day a man must fulfil the duties which grow out of his circumstances. Nor would the inward work really be prospered by the suspension or postponement of the outward. Still we say that the inward comes first; first in importance, first (in a sense) in order. No man's day's work will be interfered with by prayer and watching. On the contrary, the day is lengthened for effective labour by every moment taken from it at either end for deep communing and earnest wrestling with Him who is alike God of Nature, God of Providence, and God of Grace. Look well to the condition of that soul, the health of which, the prosperity of which, will evermore communicate itself to the work and to the life. Neglect that, and then, whatever else it may be, yours will not be the work of Faith: it will not have the

E

benediction of God: there will be nothing of it left when the thoughts of earth perish.

(2) *The work of Faith looks upward.*

Faith does not make that broad and deep line, which some draw, between religious work and unreligious. And though we have spoken of the work of Faith as beginning within, this is not to be understood as though Faith first looked to the heart and then went out to attend to the life. Faith is a thing which *moves altogether where it moves at all;* pervades everything, and makes all things of one piece and colour: insomuch that Prayer is concerned much about matters of duty and conduct, and Action, in its turn, whatever it be, draws all its strength and vitality from the Divine communion.

The work of Faith, throughout, looks upward. Not in seasons of worship only. *I have set the Lord always before me: because He is on my right hand, I shall not be moved.* The eye of Faith is upon God, even while the hand of Faith, and the foot of Faith, is moving among the things of this world.

We have scarcely yet expressed the particular thing now intended.

The motto of the work of Faith, in this aspect, is a double motto. One part of it has been given: *I have set the Lord always before me.* The other is, *I delight to do Thy will, O my God.* The one is the spiritual side, the other the practical. *God is at my right hand*—that is the strength: *My work is God's will*—that is the motive.

What assurance, what quietness, what unity, what dignity, is given to my day's work, by just remembering that, whatever it is—however humble, or however difficult—however dull, or however suffering—it is the will of God ! It is the will of God that the rich man should be bountiful, that the active man should be useful, that the public man should be patriotic, that the poor man should be provident, that the lawyer should be upright, the physician humane, the clergyman diligent. It is the will of God that I should this day go forth to my work and to my labour until the evening ; furnishing my little quota to earth's toils and to man's happiness ; serving my generation in the humble offices, at home and abroad, in which God has set me towards my fellows, until the long night cometh when I can no more work. It is the will of God that I should to-day pay this visit

of courtesy or of charity, do this act of duty or
kindness, read this book, write this letter, hold
this converse ; and I, because I have found grace
in His sight—because He has so loved me as to
give His Son to die for me, and so borne with me
and had patience as to give me this added day of
life, reason, and efficiency—I therefore *delight to do
it : Lo, I come*, like my Master before me, because
in the Volume of the Book it is prescribed to me—I
delight to do God's will, *yea, His law is within my
heart.*

Thus Faith looks upward in working.

(3) *The work of Faith looks around.*

It may be said of most, if not of all the workers
before enumerated, that their toil was in a great
degree selfish.   The work of pleasure-seeking, and
the work of money-getting, and the work of ambition, is essentially and altogether selfish.   The
work of necessity, of providing for a family, of
keeping bread in the house and hunger from the
household, has probably in it a large admixture of
selfishness : at all events, if it looks beyond itself,
it looks not beyond its own.   The work of acquir-
ing knowledge, unless it be sedulously guarded, is
commonly, if not of necessity, a self-seeking labour.

Even the work of duty—if it stops with duty—may centre in and be circumscribed by self. It is only Faith, which knows how to be really unselfish. If any of the other workers are so in any degree, it must be, we may venture to say, by an admixture, by the aid, of faith. But of faith it is written that it *worketh by love.*

How is this?

Faith says, *Let me go now to the field, and glean ears of corn after Him in whose sight I have found grace.* The work of Faith is the imitation of Christ. The work of Faith is the following and gleaning after Christ. No words could be more expressive. It is but a gleaning which is left to Faith. The work of Christ Himself is the harvest. It is He who wrought entirely by love. It is He who carried unselfishness to its limit, and left to those who come after, only, as it were, *the gleaning grapes when the vintage is done.*

But that Faith which looks within, and which looks above, does really look around also. Faith does look not only on her own things, but on the things of others. Faith does seriously contemplate the wants and the woes and the wickednesses which are making havoc of humanity, and has something truly of *that mind* in her *which was also* first and perfectly *in Christ Jesus.*

The working of Faith is through love. *By this shall all men know* that ye have faith, *if ye have love one to another.*

How is it then that any work of benevolence or charity stands still amongst us? How is it that Institutions which have the love of man for their motive, and the good of man for their object, are left imperilled and in suspense, while we *run every man to his own house,* and care not if the work of love, which is the work of God, stands still in mid course or fails to reach the goal?

In other words, *How is it that we have no faith?* for the faith which works not by love, is, in God's sight, a faith which is not.

(4) *The work of Faith looks onward.*

Whatever is not seen is an object of faith.

An Apostle teaches us that it is by faith that we apprehend even past things which we saw not. *By faith we believe that the worlds were framed by the word of God:* things seen, out of things which appear not.

And so it is by faith that we apprehend things

within, and things above, and (in a certain sense) things around also. Because, when we speak of the aspect of Faith towards things around, we speak, evidently, not of material things, but of the true interests of mankind; just of those things which make little show, which force not themselves upon notice, or which, by the nature of the case, are incapable of doing so; bodies racked by pain in secret homes, or souls endangered by sin, where the chief malady is insensibility and silence.

But most of all is faith exercised in things not only spiritual but future. *Faith is the substance (confidence) of things hoped for, the evidence of things not seen.* The work of Faith looks onward.

Oftentimes would Faith faint if it had not an onward aspect.

Faith sees at present so few results. The labour of days and weeks and months and years seems all gone for nothing. *Then I said, I have laboured in vain, I have spent my strength for nought and in vain.* Not one life seems to have been altered by many expostulations, not one soul permanently benefited by rivers of tears or by mountains of efforts. How can I carry on this lost, this thankless labour?

How can I persevere to the end in the toils of a love never repaid, never requited?

Now Faith has in itself the antidote of despair. Efforts are mine: results are God's. *Though Israel be not gathered, yet my God shall be my strength.* He never promised a speedy success. He never promised a success which the vain workman could gloat over, or a triumph which should parade itself in spirits led captive. Faith is willing to wait for the day of God's power; willing to be lost and forgotten in the eventual ingathering. *Although the fig tree shall not blossom, neither shall fruit be in the vines; the labour of the olive shall fail, and the fields shall yield no meat; the flock shall be cut off from the fold, and there shall be no herd in the stalls; yet I will rejoice in the Lord, I will joy in the God of my salvation.* Had Christ Himself counted His successes up to the moment when *He made His soul an offering for sin*, eleven poor men, and a few faithful women, would have been the sum total of His achievement. Even after the miracle of Resurrection, and the forty days of His tarrying, *the number of the names together were* but *an hundred and twenty.* Only by faith could He Himself *see of the travail of His soul and be satisfied.* Not even yet, eighteen centuries afterwards, does He see the kingdoms of this one little earth become actually the kingdoms of His reign and of His possession. He looked onward then : He looks onward still. *For the joy that was set before Him He endured the cross :* for the joy still to be revealed He endures the long ages of an intercessory priesthood, strivings of grace, and mediatorial expectation. Even thus must it be—and well may it be —with the work of Faith below. *The disciple is not above his Master.* What He counts worth the waiting for, well may we wait for, and not faint.

These all died in faith, not having received the promises. But they had *seen them afar off, and were persuaded of them, and embraced them.*

God grant us all that grace of patience, which is the very crown and glory of the work of Faith! What have we done for Christ, that we should expect to reap, while He is yet *awaiting the early and latter rain?* Looking within, that there be no rootless growth there ; looking upward, that there be no forgetfulness of the source and spring of life ; looking around, that there be no listless idling and no selfish complacency ; let us look onward also, that there be no short-sighted reckon-

ings and no irrational disappointments! Happy
is he to whom it shall be said, *Go thou thy way till
the end be: for thou shalt rest, and stand in thy lot
at the end of the days!*

IV

FAITH RESTING.

"I will lay me down in peace, and take my rest : for it is Thou,
Lord, only that makest me dwell in safety."—PSALM iv. 8.

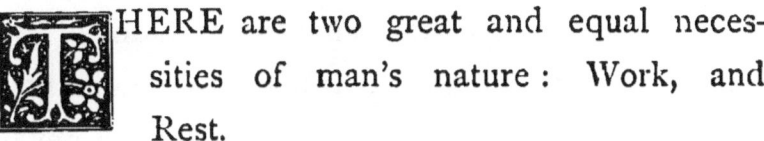HERE are two great and equal neces-
sities of man's nature : Work, and
Rest.

A man cannot be happy without either, without
both, of these. We must have work ; and we must
have rest.

Once the two things were one. An unfallen
being finds repose in activity. In Heaven *there
is no night.* The will of God is done there, not
only perfectly, but continually. Those holy spirits
which behold the face of God, and are sent forth
thence to minister to the heirs of salvation, could

do but half, not half, of their office, if they took either night or day for rest from labour. *They rest not day nor night.* They rest in working.

So shall it be, we doubt not, with us, when once the rest of the grave has removed all trace of the languors of earth, and the body of humiliation is transformed into that body of glory which never faints nor is weary either of the song of praise or of the office of love.

Meanwhile there is, for us, a divorce of the two things which God had joined together, work and rest. Work begins where rest ends : not until work is ended can rest begin. That is the condition of earth. *Man goes forth to his work and to his labour until the evening.* When night comes, *no man can work.*

We have spoken before of Nature Working, and of Faith Working. Now we are to speak of the Resting of Nature, and the Resting of Faith.

1. God our Father, merciful even to the fallen, has recognized an alternation of rest as a necessity of our being. It was God who *called the light Day*, and set the greater of the *two great lights* to rule it. And it was God who *called the darkness Night*, and

left not even night unregarded in His provision for its comfort and its beauty. *So He giveth His beloved sleep.* So He recruits exhausted energies, and testifies, not by voice but by sign, to the reality of His providence and the certainty of His judgment.

Nature rests. Night by night she lies down to sleep, guarded by a hand denied or forgotten. She too is in God's keeping: even to her He leaves not Himself without witness.

But there is a craving in man's heart for repose and relaxation, which this provision of natural sleep cannot satisfy. The want of Rest, the desire of Rest, the pursuit of Rest, lies deeper and soars higher and stretches further.

Where is the man who has not in his mind some project of rest? Not, necessarily, a rest of inaction: but at least a rest from weariness—whether it be the weariness of mere labour, or the weariness of monotony, of irksomeness, of compulsion.

The Boy looks on to his Holidays: not that he may do nothing: perhaps his holiday pursuits may be more vigorous than the occupations of School: but that he may get rid of constraints, please himself, do what he likes to do, and in that find rest.

And the man of mature age—is not he like him? Dull indeed is that life which has not some prospect, however indefinite, however remote, of repose. In early manhood, it may be the prospect of making for one's self a home—word full of rest ! of venturing upon independence and marriage ; of building a nest of safe and lawful felicity, in which all shall be concord and comfort, blessing and love. Later on, it may take the form of planning for retirement. We begin to talk of the vanity of ambition, of the unsatisfactoriness of a life drained to the dregs in business, of the comfort of having now and then a half hour of idleness, of the pleasure of being able to look forward to a little command of time, an occasional change of scene, perhaps a little enjoyment·of society, or (it may be) a little attention to the soul. At last it comes to a desire of repose, pure and simple. The old man drags himself unwillingly from his chair and his fire ; prefers the day which has no mark upon it, and the night which comes between two night-like days.

There is, I say, a prospect and a project of rest

—whatever we call rest—in all of us. What we call rest varies greatly with temperament, with circumstances, with habit, with age.

And as Rest in its simplest form is God's gift to us, and Rest in its highest form God's promise, so is Rest, in its widest sense, man's one motive; the spring of much that is noble in action, and of all that is base.

What is it which makes the Statesman careless of pleasure, the Scholar of society, the Philanthropist of money, the Missionary of home? Each is seeking rest—what he pictures as rest—what to him would be rest, might he but reach it! Fame, knowledge, good done, souls saved—each of these is a terminus—however various in value and in satisfaction: the last was so even to Him of whom Prophecy writes, *He shall see of the travail of His soul, and shall be satisfied.*

And again—to change abruptly to the very opposite—what is it which makes the spendthrift reckless of possession, the idler of success, the intemperate man of health, the immoral man of character? Is it that any one of these is really unaware of the amount which he is staking—of the utter, ruinous risk which he is running—when he yields to such habits, or even when he does the first acts which form them? No—but he is seeking rest: it is a want of his nature—and his perhaps is a low nature, and this is its idea of rest: day after day, night after night, he has the thirst of rest upon him—what we may truly call the lust of resting : and as he cannot go without his rest, and cannot wait God's time for it, or even reason's and wise men's time for it, he must seize it at once, and do yet again this thing which he knows, while he does it, to be folly and misery, sin and death.

Rest is Nature's end : and Nature makes for it in her own way; by a short road or a long one, according to her constitution, education, or caprice. If a man is wise, as man reckons wisdom, he is seeking rest: if a man is a fool, as God and man alike reckon folly, he is seeking his rest still !

2. We will leave these things here, and pass on to better. Our subject is, *Faith Resting.*

For, observe, the want of rest, and the desire of rest, and the pursuit of rest, is not wrong. God does not reprove any one of them. He only says, *This is not your rest, and this is :* this is a premature, a self-made, a fallacious and a fatal resting; and this other thing is a rest indeed for the soul, because it is a rest from Me and in Me. *Come unto me, all ye that labour and are heavy laden, and I will give you rest.* · Faith is the apprehension of that rest; the laying hold now upon the promise, the entering at last into the fruition. Faith which works is a Faith also which rests.

(1) *There is a resting of Faith which is habitual.* Faith rests while it works.

This is a peculiarity of the true Gospel. No false religion could teach it. Many human forms even of the true Gospel do not teach it. Many professed disciples of Christ Himself—men to whom the name of religious persons cannot be denied—never learn it. True faith rests habit-. ually; rests in working. It is a paradox; but a paradox full of truth, full of beauty, full of admonition.

When King Asa went out against Zerah the Ethiopian, and set the battle in array against overwhelming numbers, he cried to the Lord his God, and said, *Lord, it is nothing to Thee to help, whether with many, or with them that have no power: help us, O Lord our God; for we rest on Thee, and in*

F

Thy name we go against this multitude. Faith rested, while it wrought.

And when King Hezekiah saw the mighty host of Sennacherib coming to fight against Jerusalem, he said to his captains of war, *There be more with us than with him: with him is an arm of flesh; but with us is the Lord our God, to help us, and to fight our battles. And the people,* it is added, *rested themselves upon the words of Hezekiah king of Judah.* It was an example of faith resting (not after, but) in working.

The Gospel of Christ lays great stress upon this point. *What shall I do,* asks an awakening conscience, *to work the works of God?* Surely some great feat of self-sacrifice; some *giving of my first-born for my transgression;* some deed of self-mortification and self-crucifixion, after which the world shall be dead to me and I to the world; this surely must be the life to which God calls one who, being a sinner, would be an heir of salvation? Mark the answer. *This is the work of God, that ye believe on Him whom He hath sent.* To work is to believe. To believe is to rest. *Say not in thine heart, Who shall go up for me into heaven? or, Who shall descend for me into the deep? The word is very nigh thee. If thou shalt confess with thy mouth the Lord Jesus, and shalt believe in thine heart that God hath raised Him from the dead, thou shalt be saved.* Faith is rest.

I scarcely know which of the two sides of the truth we are more prone to forget—Faith Working, or Faith Resting. To forget the one is to disobey: to forget the other is to disbelieve. *Christ is all,* one says: then I may be idle: without exertion of mine I am safe to enter. All is done: then to do anything is to supersede Christ. Work is faith—faith is rest—rest is relief from duty: *in returning and rest ye shall be saved.* Terrible profaneness! Hence, as of course, utter carelessness, gross inconsistency, and *great occasion given to the enemies of the Lord to blaspheme.*

Another says, It is only by working with all my might that I can hope to secure an interest in Christ's salvation. If I do all my duty; if I live a life of great self-denial, of active charity, of utter unworldliness and perpetual devotion; then I may hope that God will at last accept me, give me a place in His kingdom, and set me on the right hand in the gathering of all nations. I must work as if all depended upon myself—work out my own salvation with fear and trembling—and then perhaps I shall find that Christ's merits at last cover me, and that God for His sake will forgive my sins, even mine. Words narrowly missing —but yet missing—the true tone of the Gospel! less mischievous, less pernicious, than the other, but still not the very truth itself; calculated to make life less happy, and conduct less vigorous, and religion less attractive, than God would have it to be; taking into account the one thing, Faith Working, but leaving out altogether the other, which is Faith Resting.

If Faith is to work effectually, it must rest habitually. It must rest while it works.

What does this mean?

Faith works not for salvation, but from salvation. It is not to save myself; and it is not to get a place in Christ's salvation; but it is because Christ has done all—because His work has in it the forgiveness of all sins, and the power of all workings; it is because, *if One died for all, then all died*, and live henceforth no longer to themselves but to Him who died for them and rose again— therefore it is that I work; and so working my soul rests upon Christ, even while mind and hand, strength and life, are busily occupied in working for Him.

If we would ever know real work, we must know real rest; resting from work even amidst work; resting in Christ while working for Christ.

(2) *There is a resting of Faith which is occasional.*

i. After long confusions and conflicts within, as to the true way of salvation, at last I see and I apprehend it. *Christ is all.* He has made peace. He has brought in an everlasting righteousness. In Him God is well pleased. *In Him we have redemption through His blood, the forgiveness of sins.* Can it be but that the soul, finding Him, should, for joy of that finding, rest and refresh itself, consciously, in the Lord?

ii. Doubt has returned. A book which has fallen in my way—the conversation of an unbeliever —something less palpable, a thought of unbelief, springing I know not whence within—has caused me new perplexity, new searchings of heart. What am I to think of Christ? *Art Thou He that should come?* or must I still look out, as of old, for some one who shall come—or perhaps never come—to be the Saviour of sinners and the Light of the world? At last the clouds disperse, and I see *above the brightness of the firmament* a form like that of the Son of God in heaven. The *clear shining after rain* has been vouchsafed to me, and Faith has rest and is edified.

iii. I have passed through a sore fight of temp‧tation. It seemed as though hell had opened herself for my ruin. The old days of carelessness and ungodliness never presented to me proposals so terrible. The careful and watchful and even mournful walking of months and years seemed to have gone for nothing. I found no place for the sole of my foot amidst the morasses and quagmires and precipices of unbelief, sensuality, and presump-tion, by which I was surrounded. It was as if the Saviour's history were being re-enacted in me— *I was there in the wilderness, tempted of Satan—I was with the wild beasts*—every ugly and rapacious creature, of lust and uncleanness, beset me with its howlings—*refuge failed me—I had no place to flee unto—no man cared for my soul.* In my anguish I cried to the Lord. My new weapon, All-Prayer, turned the fight in my favour: the encounter brought me to my knees—but I neither yielded, nor fled, nor fell. Then was fulfilled in me my Master's experience : *Then the devil leaveth Him, and, behold, Angels came and ministered unto Him.* After conflict, waged bravely by faith, waged manfully in Christ's name, comes of His grace a special repose : *hardly bestead and hungry*, Faith then reposes herself upon Him, and takes her rest.

iv. So is it sometimes after great labour. We have undertaken some work which is all for God. Ashamed of the idleness and self-indulgence which has so long bound and debased us ; feeling the wickedness of such a return for the self-forgetting self-sacrificing love of Christ ; seeing the days passing away, and nothing done, nothing even attempted, to bring Him one life, one soul, for His travail even unto death for us ; we did at last arouse ourselves by the help of prayer, and calling Him in went forth into the vineyard to bear something of *the burden and heat of the day.* The toil was at first difficult : flesh and blood rebelled, Satan opposed, conscience misgave me : but I persevered ; persevered unto weariness ; came back at late evening, faint and hungry : but Faith strengthened and brightened within me as I stood

before the Lord to report to Him of my poor endeavours: I found Him nearer to me when I thus
began to treat him as a Person, as One who had
work for me and would receive my reckoning:
that night I was able to say, as never before, *I will
lay me down in peace, and take my rest: for it is
Thou, Lord, only, that makest me dwell in safety.*

v. And there are restings of Faith, not in the
inward experience, but in the outward circumstances of this life.

It pleases God now and then to break the
clouds of an ordinarily monotonous or even trying
existence by a gleam of positive and lively joy.
When I have begun to say, All things are against
me—I am marked out and written down for sorrow—
I alone of all men have an unchequered unrelieved
portion of suffering—there comes something to me
—a small thing many would call it, but to me it is
not small—which stirs my stagnant pool of being
into bright, vivid, sparkling waves: the ray may
be phosphoric, meteoric, fleeting—but it served a
purpose: it said to me, Thy God, after all, is a
God of love: as often as it is safe, or as soon as
it is safe for thee, all shall be joy: wait but a
little, wait and faint not, and *thy good things* shall

replace the evil : the hand over thee is grace and goodness : soon shalt thou find it so, and that for ever. Faith rests, and is comforted.

And sometimes, on the other hand, it is not in joy, but in sorrow, that the rest comes. Are there not amongst us some who can tell of the deep peace, the entire calm, which dwells in a chamber darkened even by death? During the long days and nights of watching, it seemed hard to say, *Thy will be done.* The sight of the suffering was anguish ; the prospect of the end intolerable. But it was to be—and at last it was. The offices of the nurse and of the physician were ended together. A sad sense of uselessness seemed to settle upon the loving household. There was nothing any longer to be done : only endurance, only blank patience—and that for ever. Yet scarcely has the thought entered, than there comes with it another also. He is at rest. He is happy. No more pain—no more conflict—no more anxiety—no more sin. I shall go to him—soon at the latest. Even now we can meet in Christ. All the family, in heaven or on earth, is at one there. Faith rests—and out of bitterest sorrow draws sweetest strength.

vi. And it would be ungrateful if we added not yet one to these occasional restings of Faith: one which depends not upon any circumstance, inward or outward, of human life, but is provided everywhere, of God's goodness, in that blessed communion and fellowship which is the Church and body of Christ. When Faith droops, under the pressure of things temporal, whether adverse or prosperous, how often does it draw newness of vigour from obeying the call, *Let us go to the house of the Lord*, or the charge, *Do this in remembrance of me!* It is only presumption—it is not faith—which can dispense with these things. Christ judged better for us, as men not of the world but yet in it, when He bade us not to forsake the assembling of ourselves together, promised to be with even two or three thus gathered, and affixed a peculiar grace to the petition in which two should agree. If Faith would know what is meant by her resting, she must frequent, with earnestness and large expectation, the *table provided in the wilderness;* the feast of which it is written, that, when Jesus took bread and blessed it, and gave to them, *their eyes were opened and they knew Him.* Faith, struggling elsewhere, rests here. *Handle me, and see.*

(3) Lastly, as there is a resting which is habitual, and a resting which is occasional, so also *there is a resting of Faith which is final.*

Few words are needed to set this before us.

For we speak now of that last act of all, by which Faith is at once crowned, and dethroned; consummated, and superseded; made ripe for fruition, and swallowed up in sight.

In life it is the *work* of Faith which has predominated. Faith has had to run a race, to wage a warfare, to subdue a foe. It has had to accomplish a great task: no less than that of turning a life of nature into a life of spirit, and making a world of sense a very gate of heaven. It has had to make a poor fallen being into the preserving salt and the transforming light of its fellows. These things might be done indeed—if rightly done, they were done—in a spirit of resting: but they were themselves works of toil. Therefore during days of health and activity Faith Working has preponderated of necessity over Faith Resting.

At last sickness comes. It may be in age, or it may be in youth. Oftentimes *in the midst of life*—oftentimes in the very spring-time of life— *we are in death.* But whenever it comes—the decisive, the final sickness—it brings with it one call—one trial, one necessity, one only possibility —a call to rest. Nothing can now be done but to lie still. And is that, think we, so easy ? Visit a bed of death, and see whether even patience, whether even submission—much more, whether affiance, whether faith—is the grace of every man! O, we see then the truth of the saying, *And that not of yourselves, it is the gift of God !* To rest on the Lord then, is just as *impossible with man* as it is in life to work for God.

But faith—the man of faith—can do it. He thinks this one of the chief blessings, one of the chief evidences too, of Christ's Gospel, that it never sets a man to do anything impossible ; that its demand is always appropriate ; its call exactly suitable to youth and age, to health and sickness, to life and to death. To him now it says only these two words, *Faith, rest!* Lie still, and look upward. What has been left undone cannot now be done : rest it upon Christ. What has been ill done cannot now be amended : rest it upon Christ. What has been done amiss cannot now be undone : rest it upon Christ. Lean all thy weight upon Him. He is sufficient. He has borne all. Trust Him, and doubt not. He will undertake for thee. It is enough.

And so that Faith which has rested habitually —that Faith which has rested occasionally— rests now finally. *My flesh shall rest in hope. I shall be satisfied, when I awake, with Thy likeness. I will both lay me down in peace, and sleep*—sleep, God willing it, the long sleep—*for it is Thou, Lord, only, that makest me dwell in safety. All live unto Thee* —the dead and the living. Death does but withdraw the veil, the slight thin veil, between the seen and the unseen, between sense and spirit, between the soul and Christ. I shall *dwell in safety* still, if I *sleep in Jesus.*

The restings of Faith are ended: the rest of sight is begun.

V

FAITH FIGHTING.

"When I cry unto Thee, then shall mine enemies turn back : this I know ; for God is for me."—PSALM lvi. 9.

IFE is at once a field of work and a field of battle. It is so for Nature : it is not less so for Grace. The Faith which works is a Faith also which fights. *Every one with one of his hands wrought in the work, and with the other hand held a weapon.* The same Apostle who wrote to one of his congregations, *I remember your work of faith,* wrote also to one of his friends, *Fight the good fight of faith,* and so *lay hold on eternal life.*

Faith Working describes but one-half of life's whole activity. Now we are to add the other: *Faith Fighting.*

1. *From whence come wars and fightings among*

you? St James asks—asks of a nominally Christian community—and answers this question by another: *Come they not hence, even of your lusts that war in your members?*

Thus he introduces to us the thought of Nature fighting; and warns us too that Nature may fight still even in those who by profession and privilege are children of grace.

There are two fruitful sources of discord in the world, heathen or Christian, of the fallen Adam. They might be traced, doubtless, up to one. But in practice they are distinguishable: Selfishness, and Pride. St Paul deals with both of them in his Epistle to the Philippians. He speaks of those who *seek their own*, and charges Christian people not to look on their own things, but also on the interests of others. He speaks also of doing things *through vainglory;* and bids Christians *in lowliness of mind to esteem each the other as better than themselves.* And these two cautions he connects with his call to unity. In other words, he points out selfishness and pride as the two chief sources of Nature's fightings.

(1) There is an object in view, attainable but by one, and two would have it.

It may be office—it may be emolument—it may be honour.

Hence, at once, discord. Out of selfishness fightings. Eagerness, ambition, covetousness, party-spirit, efforts to outstrip by interest or to trip up by calumny, to circumvent by intrigue or to damage by slander—and a whole world of warfare is instantly kindled by throwing into it one spark of that provocation which is the self, the fallen self, of Nature.

And so in a thousand smaller or less visible workings.

Every trade, every profession, every social circle, has its own selfishnesses, and as a necessary consequence its own fightings. In a certain sense, in all these things, every man's hand is against his brother's. Every man's gain is another's loss. One man cannot succeed, but another suffers. And although there is a Christian way of bearing these defeats, and even of subduing these dispositions—and a worldly way also, either imitated from the Christian, or else framed upon calculations of self-interest and personal comfort, preventing the display or even the fostering of those enmities which spring and strive and war

within—still there is also, on the whole, a vast
amount of commercial and professional and social
jealousy seething below the calm surface of conventional propriety, and from time to time sending to the surface one of those bubbles of rancor-
ous bickering, which may be evanescent in their
nature, but are at least noisy in the explosion and
mischievous in the consequences.

Selfishness fights.

(2) And Pride too has its fightings.

How many of our divisions are distinctly trace-
able to it!

A person thinks himself slighted. He has not
been consulted, as he ought to have been, on some
practical question. Or he was not consulted first,
or perhaps not last. Or, though consulted, he was
not followed. An adverse or a different opinion
prevailed. Or, in consultation, some disparaging
half-contemptuous expression was dropped by another. I had no reply ready, and the success
rested with him. Pride was wounded, and dis-
comfort, soreness, unfriendliness, was the result.
From whence come wars and fightings among you?
Often from wounded pride.

Or not in business but in society offence has

been given and taken. Some one else took pre-
cedence of me in a festive gathering. The host
gave it him. As small a thing as this has caused
a breach and a hostility! Or some one has been
wanting in paying me the courtesy of a visit, or in
returning the civility of mine. Or a slighting word
was dropped, the other day, concerning me in the
house of a friend—dropped, and not resented.
Or an idle tale was told of me, by one who ought
to have known better. Or a change of manner is
perceptible in some one towards me, which can pro-
ceed, certainly, from nothing but from having heard
something against me. Pride broods over the suspicion, and nurses it into a settled resentment.
The ignorant, unsuspecting, innocent cause is
never told of it, and sleeps securely upon the vol-
cano of his own unconscious kindling!

I have only just prefaced my real subject with
these experiences of the life of this world, because
they serve to illustrate, by contrast, the soul's warfare, and to show us how different is the use which
Christ would have us make of that principle of
combativeness and of pugnacity which the heavenly
Artificer set in us from the beginning.

It is not wrong to fight—but with whom? in

what armour? with what weapons? for what prize?

2. *Fight the good fight of faith.*

Volumes might be written, and the subject scarcely touched still.

Take into view just three particulars.

(1) *Faith descrying.*

Celebrated pictures of great commanders show them to us in the use of the telescope or descrying-glass. They are looking out. They are observing the enemy. They cannot plan, they can still less act, till they see the foe and his dispositions. It is so with Faith.

We have seen what are the foes of Nature. They are those persons who threaten to interfere with my earthly interests. They are those persons who have disparaged, or whom I suspect of wishing to disparage, my honour, or importance, or ability, or worldly position. Are these the foes of Faith?

Faith, which is the sight of the unseen, may be expected to discern, through her descrying-glass, a different kind of antagonists from those whom Nature, fallen Nature, discovers by her reconnoitring. And it is so.

We wrestle, St Paul says, *not against flesh and blood.* The confounding, still more the interchanging, of friend and foe, has been in all times a fruitful source of defeat. In the mist of the foggy November morning the soldiers of England at Inkermann could not at first know the Russian from the Frenchman. And the position itself might have been sacrificed to that confusion. It is just so in the conflict between the human soul and its enemies.

All tempters approach us in disguise. If we could see their features as God and good Angels see them, there would be in them no attractions. We should see in the smile of love the grin of malice : we should perceive in the *word smoother than oil,* the *very sword* of hatred and hostility.

But of this discernment Nature is incapable. That which offers me present indulgence must be my friend. That which tells me unwelcome truths must be my foe.

We might almost say that Faith reverses this judgment. So much reason has she for suspicion of present seeming, that she almost says, I may judge of friend and foe inversely by the profession. It was to Elijah that Ahab said, *Hast thou found me, O mine enemy?* He said not so to Jezebel.

Faith Fighting is, first of all, Faith descrying.

Now when Faith sets herself thus to discriminate friend and foe, she perceives but one real enemy, and that is Sin. She does not wage war with flesh and blood. Faith does not bid me to count as my enemy the man who has gained this or that prize for which I had been a candidate—not this or that person who has outrun me in the race of this world—this commercial, or that professional, or that social rival, whose business has prospered beyond mine, whose skill or whose talent has been acknowledged by a wider circle or a more unanimous verdict. That is Nature's foe possibly : but it is not the antagonist of Faith. Faith sees in such persons a friend in disguise. One who has been ordained of God to humble pride, to reprove self-confidence, and to make vanity in its own eyes contemptible. The one enemy of Faith is Sin.

But the armies of that one enemy are marshalled under three chief captains. And though the word of command is one, and the object of the war one, and the plan of campaign also one, still Faith finds it necessary to recognize a division too, and to prepare herself for the conflict in different departments and aspects.

i. The first of these is the world. The gaze of Faith being stedfastly fixed upwards and onwards—upward toward the throne of God, onward toward the eternal future—she must, of course, regard as hostile any influence which drags her downwards, and any influence which enchains her in the present. Now it is the one object of the world to effect this. The sin of the world is not in saying that that is pleasant which is not pleasant, or that painful which is not painful. Faith does not expect the world to say that a life of obscurity and dulness is more enjoyable or more attractive than a life of eminence and bustle and public fame. It would be a falsehood if it did say so. The error of the world, and the falsehood of the world, lies in bidding us choose the pleasanter and the easier, in place of the more difficult and the more enduring. The sin of the world consists in making the seen and the temporal more real and more important than the invisible and the eternal.

That then is the first of the foes of Faith. And observe, it needs Faith to descry it as such. Any one except the man of Faith would view it differently; would hail as a friend and an auxiliary that which Faith repels as an enemy in disguise.

ii. Just so is it with the second—the flesh. Faith is well aware that it is more pleasant to humour the flesh than to crucify it. More pleasant to sit still and enjoy, than to go forth and labour. More pleasant to imbibe the sweet syrup of lust, than to refuse and repel it as a honeyed poison. More pleasant to live luxurious days and sleep delicious nights, than to rise early and late take rest, in doing the work of God, and bearing forth upon the shoulder the sharp cross of Christ. Faith is as necessary to descry this foe as to encounter it.

iii. And the devil. Does he come, did he come in Paradise, as an open enemy—as one who brings fire in his hand, and hell in his promise? Is it more pleasant, at the moment, to think a devil's thought —of resentment, of anger, of malice, of revenge—or to repel it? Is it more pleasant, at the moment, to retaliate or to forgive a wrong—to say the bitter word, to vent the angry retort, or to suppress it—to utter the convenient lie which suggested itself, or to smother and bury it, and say the truth? Is it always easy, on the instant, to keep down the thought of murmuring and discontent at God's dealings with you in his Providence or in His grace—to refuse to think of Him as a hard taskmaster or a relentless judge—to say, as each new anxiety arises, *Thy will be done*—or, as every successive stroke falls, *He doeth all things well?*

It is Faith—it is not Nature—which descries the real foe under the pretended friend, and wages war, not with flesh and blood—not with an irksome duty, and not with an unwelcome Providence—but rather with sinful inclination, with a perverse will, and with *spiritual wickednesses in high places.*

(2) *Faith arming.*

When Faith has descried her foe, she must prepare to meet him.

And special directions are given her with a view to this preparation.

Take unto you, St Paul says, *the whole armour of God, that ye may be able to withstand in the evil day.*

One or two things must be noticed.

i. Faith must arm before the battle.

Many persons say, It will be time enough to resist when temptation comes.

St Paul says, He who waits to arm himself till then, will be defeated and captured.

ii. The armour of Faith—with one, if one, exception—consists of habits; principles of good—in other words, graces of the Spirit—which he who would have once must have always.

A person says, How hard that I should fall, when I prayed so earnestly!

Yes, but were you armed beforehand? Was the habit of your life Christian? Or did you expect to get straight and direct from God's treasure-house, for one single wearing, armour which you had never essayed and never proved?

iii. Look then at the armour. Not to discourage—but to humble, and to instruct.

Truth. The loins girt about with truth. We understand by this, sincerity. Reality of character: earnestness of purpose: thoroughness of devotion. Many have all save just this. Many regrets, many resolutions: strong impulses, fervent aspirations, zealous endeavours: only just not Truth. The girdle which binds all together is wanting: the garments hang loose and discinct· the man rushes into the battle, not one but many.

Righteousness. *Having on the breastplate of righteousness.* Ah! some would put instead of this—what is more easily fancied or counterfeited—the imputation of a theological justification! No wonder! But what Faith wants for her breastplate, is something which may indeed spring out of this — which can only spring out of a living trust in the completed work of Christ—yet *is* not this. It is that safeguard —practically speaking — of an habitual endeavour *to have always a conscience void of offence towards God and man,* which St Paul is not afraid to call here the Christian breastplate, and elsewhere, yet more strongly, *the armour of righteousness on the right hand and on the left.*

Readiness. *Your feet shod with the preparation (readiness) of the Gospel of peace.*

One man wants the girdle—another the breastplate—another the sandals. To how many a man, not otherwise unhopeful, might we give the old surname of *the Unready!* I ought to have seized the opportunity—but it escaped me. I ought to have availed myself of that opening for a word of counsel—but I was not ready, and the door closed. I ought to have answered on the instant that taunt, that innuendo, of the infidel—but I was not ready: the conversation changed before I spoke, and the honour of Christ my Lord lay there unvindicated. I ought to have hastened to that bed of sickness, to that house of mourning: but I was not ready, and before I went, sickness was again health, or sorrow was again forgetfulness.

So with the rest. Each part of the armour—I have spoken but of three parts—must be put on beforehand; before the battle begins; before that fiery trial which will try every man's faith of what sort it is.

(3) *Faith engaging.* Faith in conflict.

The foe is ascertained—and faith is armed to meet him. The moment of action is come.

This action itself may be twofold. There is the action of defence, and there is the action of aggression. Faith may await the onset—or Faith herself may charge.

i. Faith defensive is Faith tempted.

Holy Scripture abounds in examples of the conflict of Faith with the tempter.

There is the noble Hebrew youth resisting the solicitations of a wicked Egyptian matron, with the unanswerable, the impregnable question, *How can I do this great wickedness, and sin against God ?*

There is the great Hebrew lawgiver learning in early manhood the lesson of future strength, when he *refuses to be called the son of Pharaoh's daughter, because he counts the reproach of Christ greater riches than the treasures of Egypt, having respect to the recompense of the reward.*

There are the three faithful Israelites under the shadow of the giant empire of Babylon, refusing to worship the great golden image, because they know that the God whom they serve can, if He will, deliver them from the fiery furnace—and because, if not, if He wills not to deliver them, they can obey and trust Him still.

There is the heroic Hebrew Prophet firm to worship God as he did aforetime, because, though *the writing is signed against him,* he cannot forego the wonted communion, and knows that, if he be given to death here, he shall *obtain a better resurrection.*

These are all examples of Faith Fighting.

And there is one greater still.

Our Lord Jesus Christ, coming to bear all our

sorrows, must be *in all points tempted like as we
are.* In body, in soul, in spirit—by appetite, by
ambition, by presumption—in the most insidious
because the most refined and elevated of all forms
—He is subjected to the influence of temptation.
To change stones into bread for his own support ;
to take to Himself the kingdoms of the earth,
and reign at once ; to rely upon the protecting
care of God, and *for the more confirmation of
the faith* cast Himself unhurt from the pinnacle
of the Temple ; such is the temptation which
Faith, in Him, endured and vanquished ; vanquished not more in our stead than as our example ; vanquished each time in the strength of
that Word of God, which is, for us also, the one
offensive weapon — *the sword of the Spirit,* two-
edged, and *turning every way,* for the discomfiture
of the tempter and the protection of the soul.

It is with the defensive warfare of Faith that
we are all primarily concerned. For one man
who has to wage any aggressive warfare, a thousand and ten thousand must repel for their
souls' sake the assaults of the devil. And where
amongst us is he who can do this? Even of
Christian men how many stand upright when Satan

strongly assails? Who is there who does not mix together too often the allurements of inclination and the promises of the Gospel—weakly yield or timidly flee when sin tempts, and only hope afterwards that, nevertheless, God will forgive?

Not so does Faith. She calls in the help of God, and knows that, when she calls, her enemies will be put to flight, because God Himself, the Almighty, is on her side.

It is indeed chiefly thus—chiefly by earnest, resolute, determined Prayer—that Faith itself conquers. *Praying always, with all prayer and supplication in the Spirit, and watching thereunto with all perseverance.* We have spoken of the previous arming; of those principles and habits of the soul which must be formed in us and fostered before the special conflict begins. But how are these habits of grace themselves formed in any man? Is it not by daily, by persevering prayer—prayer begun in much weakness, amidst many wanderings of thought and many interruptions of unbelief—but adhered to, and persisted in, till at last an answer came — an answer of hope and peace within, an answer of help and strength without? And of what avail would even habits of grace be, in the emergency of a strong temptation, without a present God, and without a real grace, called in and apprehended at the moment by special, eager, importunate prayer? A man of Faith must be a man of Prayer. By prayer he believes, and by prayer prevails : prayer is the very link between faith and God, between the soul that is all weakness and the God who is Omnipotent strength. *My grace is sufficient for thee : for my strength is made perfect in weakness.*

ii. But is Faith then, Christian faith, to be always and altogether defensive? Is it enough that she should repel attack, and never wage, herself, an aggressive warfare?

It would be well indeed if none allowed themselves to attack, who have not first learned to repel. It would be well, if only they advanced to the decisive, the final charge, who had first tried, in themselves, the temper of their Divine weapon, and found it all-sufficient to save themselves from death.

But when this is done ; when the life has been redeemed and cleansed from sin ; when the soul is given to the Lord who bought it, to be a living and a life-long sacrifice to His glory; then there must be something done—ill were it for the world else—to carry the war into the enemy's country; to *show forth the praises of Him who hath called us out of darkness into His marvellous light*, by the living example of a holy life, and by the persuasive influence of a consistent devotion. Faith must not repel only—she must at last charge also.

Where should we have been—where would have been this Church of England, with her ordinances of worship and her influences of good—if the first Apostles of truth had been faithful only in resisting temptation—if they had never risen to the help of the Lord against a mighty world and a mightier spirit of evil?

It is not enough, anywhere or in any age, that we live in the enjoyment of Christian privileges, and think not how to hold out the lamp of life to the millions still sitting in darkness. What are we doing—what am I doing, let each one ask himself —to make the warfare of faith not defensive only but aggressive too?

And this I say, brethren, the time is short. Let each one set himself something—if it be but a little thing—in the way of a warfare to be waged in Christ for God. God gives us a wide choice of our field of service : only let us all enlist ourselves under His banner, and in some manner, and in some place—at home or abroad—in the cause of piety or of charity—in the service of the evangelization of our country, or of its rescue from some of the terrible moral evils which drag it down unto perdition—set ourselves to *fight the good fight of faith,* and to *lay hold,* in so doing, *on eternal life.*

So at last — when our time comes, and the shadows of earth must be exchanged for the realities unseen—ours shall be the experience written down for all time by the great Apostle and Evangelist of nations, *I have fought a good fight, I have finished my course, I have kept the faith : henceforth there is laid up for me a crown of righteousness, which the Lord, the righteous Judge, shall give me at that day;* the day of the restitution and the refreshing— of the final discomfiture of evil, and the everlasting triumph of good.

VI

FAITH CONQUERING.

"He shall overcome at the last."—GEN. xlix. 19.

IN the race of life there are many runners for one victor. In the battle of life there are many combatants for one conqueror.

Every generation, every profession, every place, almost every family, has its disappointed men as well as its successful. Wide as the world is, it is not wide enough for a universal success: there must be obscurity, there must be failure, there must be defeat, or the race of man would be an army of generals, with none to follow them, and none to obey.

Now, is there any characteristic quality which either prognosticates or explains a career of earthly success? Is there any sense in which we can speak of Nature Conquering, so as to furnish an illustration, whether in the way of likeness or contrast, of our present subject, which is *Faith* Conquering?

A man looking back, from middle or later life, upon the companions of his boyhood, will not only be ready to moralize upon their fortunes, but able also, roughly at least, to generalize and account for them.

He will recall one, perhaps, who had singular advantages of mind, of body, and of estate. He was the envy and admiration of his fellows : quickness of apprehension, versatility of intellect, readiness of expression, wonderful health, spirits, and activity ; in addition to these, high birth, an ample fortune, a wide circle of friends—everything in possession, and everything in prospect to secure success : where is he now? Outstripped in the race by competitors whom once he despised ; ruined, long years past, slowly by indolence, or suddenly by vice ; pitied now as he once was envied ; or not even pitied—just put aside, passed by, overlooked, and forgotten.

So then none of these things are securities for

success, speaking at present only of this world's struggles. A man may have every gift of nature, and yet be, even in these competitions, nowhere and nothing.

Another, little known and little noticeable in youth, has risen to great eminence. He has utterly baffled the calculations of early friends: they can scarcely reconcile themselves to a reversal so complete of their expectations and judgments. At each step of his advancement they have talked of accident; of the chances of life, and the caprices of fortune. And yet, perhaps, if we knew all, we should scarcely find any place at all in human life for such influences as these. On reflection, you will probably find that that man of unlooked-for success had in him at least three qualities, the sum of which in their developed maturity was the cause (humanly speaking) and the sufficient explanation of his triumph.

The first of these was resolution. That man could set before himself an object. He did not run uncertainly, nor in fighting did he beat the air. He saw distinctly the goal for which he would start, and the nature of the prize which hung upon it. He willed, he resolved, he determined, to succeed. He did not allow himself to multiply or to change his objects. His motto was, *This one thing I do.* This thing is my choice, and to this I will adhere. Resolution.

The second quality was good sense. He sought his one end by prudent means. He did not allow himself to be misled by appearances nor diverted by speculations. He judged with calm and steady gravity what would, and what would not, day by day, advance him towards his end. There were many who said to him, This is the way: this bypath will be a short cut to your object: this present offer will shorten your toil by years, and bring you at once to notice and to distinction. He knew better. Good sense guided each step, as resolution had set him in the way.

The third quality was perseverance. As he knew that the way was long, he was not daunted by finding it so. He was prepared for delays, he was prepared for difficulties; he was prepared for impediments, and he was prepared for disappointments. He took these as things of course. They did not shake his resolution, and they did not affect his expectation. He would succeed still, for all that. Toil long and patient, toil constant and arduous, was to him but one of the conditions upon which he started in the race of life. Without perseverance he would have failed, whatever his resolution and whatever his good sense. The three together form one of those triple cords of which the wise man says that they are not quickly broken. The three together form that character which Christ Himself set in sorrowful contrast with that of too many of His own disciples, when He said, *The children of this world are in their generation wiser than the children of light.*

And we might go on to speak, not of the successes of this life, but of other achievements and conquests, of which nevertheless it must be said that they are victories not of grace but of nature.

For example.

Pride will cast out many sins. There are many weaknesses and many meannesses over which pride will gain an easy success. Many a lust of the flesh has been precluded, or else broken off, by wounded self-love or mortified vanity. A man will not stoop to accept an unwilling affection : a man will not demean himself to solicit where he has been refused or slighted. There is such a thing as Pride Conquering.

And Ambition will cast out many sins. A man bent upon being the great man of his generation will not waste himself upon light trivialities of worldliness or loose extravagances of passion: he will reserve himself for higher things, and not risk for minor self-indulgences the attainment of his real end, his great prize—it also of the earth and earthly! There is such a thing as Ambition Conquering.

And Affection, lawful love, will cast out many sins. A man without religion will be kept faithful by a sincere attachment. A man who fears not God will forfeit comfort, will risk life itself, for the defence or rescue of wife or child. Selfishness has been overborne and vanquished by a mightier force of love. It is not Divine love only, it is sometimes human love and earthly, which is mighty and all-prevailing. There is such a thing as Affection Conquering.

And yet, great as are the achievements of nature, they are as nothing in comparison with the victories of grace. At the best they are bounded by time: at the best they win a corruptible crown. Turn from them to look at our present subject — which is Faith Conquering.

See what Faith conquers, and see how Faith conquers: and then we shall understand the saying that is written, *Whatsoever is born of God overcometh the world: and this is the victory that overcometh the world, even our faith.*

Faith Conquering.

Out of a vast subject we must select just a few particulars.

1. Faith triumphant in Doubt.

The Gospel is a Revelation. It is the telling of a secret. It is the clearing away of mists and clouds which hang around man's destiny and God's purpose. It is the bringing of life and immortality to light. It is the disclosure of a mystery buried in silence from eternal times. Never let us so speak as if the Gospel had added to man's perplexities, or made that dark or darker which was light or comparatively light before. These are representations of the matter, at once ungrateful and false. The mysteries of the Gospel are all, so far as they go, revelations. They are all, so far as they go, secrets told, not secrets kept. There is not one mystery—in the human sense of the word—either about man or about God, which has been either caused or aggravated by the Gospel. Doubtless there are matters not yet revealed. There are unexplained, perhaps inexplicable, difficulties, as regards God's will and man's future, which the Gospel leaves where it found them. It is of the very nature of sin and a Fall to create such difficulties. And God might give us ten Gospels, and not remove these. All we say is, that the Gospel of Christ causes none of these, and clears away many.

Many, but not all. So many as lay really in the way of man's access to God; but not those which lay in the way of man's speculations about God. That is the distinction. God by the Gospel taught us the way of salvation: but God did not teach us, by any of His revelations, that which might have gratified curiosity, but which it could not assist duty, to know concerning Himself.

More than this. Every fresh accession of light not only leaves a fringe and border of darkness around it, but makes us more conscious of the extent and of the density of that darkness. Therefore it is that many questions trouble an enquiring Christian, which do not seem to have troubled an enquiring Jew. The very fact of knowing so much makes us impatient of not knowing more. A thousand questions remain unanswered concerning the power of God, the justice of God, and the goodness of God, which all the more exercise the patience or even burden the conscience of a Christian, because God has told him so much, and because Christ has come to be the Light of the World and the Justifier of the ways of God to man.

Now Faith, the sight of the invisible—Christian faith, which is the sight of the invisible God in Christ—must needs have an office to discharge in reference to these difficulties and these perplexities. It was so from the beginning. The Apostles themselves felt this, when they were first called to believe in the possibility, in the fact, of a Resurrection. *When they saw Him, they worshipped Him : but some doubted.* Did they not worship? Did doubt preclude faith? Rather faith triumphed in and over doubting: and they who could not explain, and they who could not understand, yet felt themselves to be in the presence of a mightier and more convincing reality, and even where they could not see they could adore and they could believe still !

So is it now. A man keenly sensible of difficulties—a man on whose very soul lie the burdens
of a thousand unreconciled contradictions—a man
who feels that he would give all that he possesses
for one ray of solution and of explanation—is no
hypocrite, and no unbeliever, if he still calls Christ
his Saviour, offers before Him all the powers and
dedicates to Him all the capacities of his being.
His doubts are as nothing in comparison with his
evidences. Is he to give up Christ, and go back into
the outer darkness of sin unforgiven and heaven unopened, because he cannot fathom the deep abyss
of a Trinity in Unity, or combine in one logical
theory the two opposite necessities, of a responsible man and an Omnipotent God? If he can
find a lamp for his feet and a light for his steps ;
if he can find a Saviour worthy of his devotion,
and a Spirit omnipresent to guide ; he must be content to wait for explanations till he reaches a land
where there is neither temptation nor weakness ;
a life in which the intellect may expand itself in
God's presence, and the soul drink in knowledge
at the fountainhead of God's truth. In the mean-
time faith triumphs amidst doubtings ; and when

Christ asks, *Will ye also go away?* is content to answer, *Lord, to whom shall we go? Thou hast the words of eternal life.*

2. Faith triumphant in Disappointment.

It is the natural thought of one who enters seriously upon a life of faith, that of course faith will conduct him straight to victory. He has only to call Christ in, and success must be sure. Whether he set himself to the conquest of sin or to the performance of duty; whether he wrestle with a besetting temptation, or gird on his armour for conflict with opposing wickednesses; in either, in any case, if the Gospel be true, he will find himself strong for victory. And thus he goes forth into the battlefield of life, outward or inward; begins his warfare with pride, with evil temper, with murmuring, with indolence, with sin, with self; or else, at the appointed hour, sets himself to seek, abroad, the opposing demon of carelessness or ungodliness, of intemperance or cruelty; visits the homes of the poor, full of the sincere desire to carry into them the illuminating light, the irresistible power, of Christ's Gospel; nothing doubting, that his Master still lives, still works, as swift to hear as He is strong to save. But what is the issue? Within, it is as though what before was an influence, became now a possession, of evil : never till he began to resist did he feel what was the strength, what the malignity, what the pertinacity, of sin. It seems almost as though his prayers were answered by contraries ; as if, when he asked for strength, he was endued with weakness ; when he implored victory, he was recompensed with defeat. Never before was he so severely tempted; never before did he more shamefully fall. Evil temper, evil desire, sinful indolence, repugnance to duty—each in its turn seems to be let loose upon him, *as it were a ramping and a roaring lion.* More than ever before, *when he would do good, evil is present with him.* In attempting, such as he is, to do any work of good for others— whether it be to teach the young, or to minister to the sick, or to reason and remonstrate with the wicked—he is ready to call himself a hypocrite and a deceiver. What is he, that he should work the work of God? And in attempting that work, what does he effect? What becomes of his labour? Can he point to one home brightened, one life altered, or one soul saved, by his ministry? It is discouragement, disappointment, defeat, every part of it. If he looks within, all is weakness and darkness : if he looks without, all is lost labour, mere vanity and vexation of spirit.

But Faith, if it be Faith, triumphs still. Triumphs amidst, and triumphs over, baffled hopes and wasted toils. That is because it is Faith. If we walked by sight, of course results would be everything. That which succeeded not, that which was not seen to succeed, would be as if it were not. But Faith, the realization of things future, and the sight of things unseen, is no respecter of present recompenses. A man of faith may be daunted, but not Faith itself. He is daunted for lack of faith. The promise has regard not only or chiefly to this life, but to the life to come. To be willing to wait, even for encouragement, much more for victory, is an essential part of his character who has *seen the promise afar off, and been persuaded of it, and embraced it,* and who now lives day by day in the calm humble looking-for of a light that shall arise and a rest that is reserved in heaven for God's people.

Whether the disappointment be inward or outward ; in the soul, or in the life ; in the life of feeling, or in the life of action ; it is the office of faith to conquer and to triumph still—assured that God's time will come, and that He is faithful still who promised.

3. But let us not leave it in doubt—for it were but a false and fallacious comfort to do so— whether faith is, even in the present, a power or a weakness. ·Something that has been said might be so interpreted as to represent faith as the discoverer rather than the conqueror of indwelling sin. And indeed there is a truth there also. The letting in of God's light upon the darkened chamber of the careless and sin-bound soul, must have the first effect of disclosing the disorder and the impurity within. That too is an office of faith. But the words, Faith Conquering, would have little hope and little meaning in them for sinners, if we could not speak of it, first, and above all, as conquering Sin. That is our most urgent want, and that is Faith's most solemn office. It is not because of his faith that any man remains the slave of his sins. It is not because he trusts in the blood of Christ to save him in them and amidst them and under them still. That is a terrible perversion of the Gospel of free grace. *Shall we continue in sin, that grace may abound?* St Paul asks. *God forbid! How shall we that are dead to sin live any*

longer therein ? It is the office of faith to make us
see Christ ; see Him in His death for our forgiveness, see Him in His life after death for our sanctification. Was any man ever encouraged in his
sins by looking up into heaven, and discerning
there at the right hand of God the form of Christ
crucified and Christ risen? Was any man ever
made indifferent to the result of his day's conflict
with his own sins, by meditating upon the all-suffi-
ciency of the sacrifice, or upon the freeness and
fulness of the Divine absolution? Nay, is there
not in all these things a motive and an influence
and a strength too, directly conducive to a watchful and a praying and a holy life? Faith Conquering is, above all things, Faith conquering sin ;
Faith looking upwards to a living Saviour, and
drawing down from Him the desire and the effort
and the grace to be holy. It is true, Faith is
seen in never despairing under the disappointment
of this hope : Faith is seen in looking upward still,
even if no answer comes : Faith is seen in determining, even if God be silent—even if Christ should
say, *It is not meet to take the children's bread and
cast it to dogs*—still to submit, still to struggle, and
still to pray. But it is a higher exercise of Faith

to draw down the blessing itself by continued, by importunate supplication. The Syrophœnician woman went not back to her house acquiescing in her disappointment : faith triumphed over the disappointment, and made her ask on against refusal, and hope on against hope, till the answer of peace came, which said, *Be it unto thee even as thou wilt.* If faith does not at last conquer sin, its other victories will be turned at last into discomfitures.

Let this question sound in the secret depth of each heart, *Is faith conquering sin in me ?* Am I indeed striving against sin ? And that, not from pride, and not from self-interest, and not from the ambition to be tranquil and self-satisfied within— but from faith ? from believing in Jesus Christ? from the desire to please Him, to be like Him, at last to be with Him ? God grant that we shrink not, any of us, from the question ! It is our life. A man who is using faith to conquer sin, must be a Christian man : he has God's mark upon him : he shall one day be at rest in heaven. Any one else—any one who is not resisting sin, or not resisting it by the help of faith—may have many things ; may be amiable, acceptable, useful ; may even be talking of the Gospel, and hoping to be saved, and making his boast of Christ: but he lacks the one thing needful: he has still to deny himself, and take up his cross and follow Jesus.

4. Conquering doubt, conquering disappointment, conquering sin, there is yet one more enemy for faith to conquer—and that is Death.

There is a strange confidence in some of us concerning that end (or, if the Gospel be true, that beginning) of being, which we call Death. We must all die, we say: as if the universality made it safe, and the necessity easy. And yet, when we reflect upon it, how mysterious, how formidable, how awful a thing, is death! What have we to rely upon, in taking that plunge into the invisible? Surely the inevitableness is not comfort? What is beyond? Where shall we be, and what, when that brief or that protracted struggle is ended—when the body has become a corpse, and the ministrations of the sick-room are exchanged for the solemn silence of the chamber of death? Where shall I—the real personal being—find myself then? where, and what? Surely if there be anywhere any information to be found upon this subject, it must demand my study! And if there be any one who can tell me that he has gone through this, and that he

knows the great secret, and that he can counsel
me how to prepare for death and how to die—
surely I must listen! And still more if there be
One Person, who not only knows, and can instruct,
and can counsel, but who also can offer to be with
me in dying, and to support me through death, and
to meet me beyond death, and to be my Friend and
my Rest and my Happiness in that eternal age of
which for myself I know and can know nothing—
surely nothing can compare in importance with the
acquisition and with the cementing and with the
enjoyment of this knowledge, this friendship, this
communion of an everlasting love! If I can become
acquainted with this Person now—if I can grow into
loving Him—if I can find peace now in receiving
His Spirit to be my spirit, and in taking His will for
my will, and His work and His objects to be mine
also—so that time and eternity may be linked together, for me, by a real unity of interest and
occupation—and death, instead of being a wrench
and a disruption, may be nothing more than 'the
drawing aside of a curtain, or the entering through
a long closed door into the very presence of One
whom, not having seen, I have already loved and
already lived for—if all this may be, then I am

justified in saying that death, the last enemy, is, for me, by anticipation vanquished—I can exclaim already, without a sense of presumption and without a fear of disappointment, *O death, where is thy sting? O grave, where is thy victory? Thanks be to God which giveth me the victory through our Lord Jesus Christ!*

And this conquest of death is, from first to last, a victory of faith. Dreadful must it be, if that is all that I know of it, to undergo, through pain and anguish, amidst misgivings of mind and lamentations of surrounding friends, a change which must separate me from all that is seen, and carry me into a region dark, blank, and friendless. If death is not this to the Christian, to what does he owe the difference? Simply to the fact that in that other world—as we vaguely term it—there is already, for him, a Father and a Saviour and a Comforter—One whom it has been the joy of his soul to commune with here, and the strength of his life to find real, to find near, and to find all love and strength and grace.

Now therefore the workings of Faith are accomplished. If Faith can conquer death, it has conquered the last enemy. There is none be-

yond. He who can die well has done all. Beyond
death, there is nothing new. Earth's doubtings
are vanquished, and earth's disappointments are
vanquished, and earth's sins are vanquished, if
death is vanquished for me! Let us not be de-
ceived about this. Let us not come to the brink
of that river, and then find that we cannot cross
it! Let us not plunge into that stream, to sink
and drown there! If we would die happy, we
must first be holy. If we would be indeed holy,
we must first be Christ's.

Christ Himself upon earth condescended to
walk by Faith. His victories were victories of
Faith.

He conquered Doubt by Faith. Whom did
doubt ever assail as it assailed Him? On the
cross he cried aloud, *My God, my God, why hast
Thou forsaken me?* So far as Scripture tells,
there was no lightening of that load even to the
last breath. And yet His words were, *Father,
into Thy hands I commend my spirit.*

And Christ conquered Disappointment by
Faith. Was it nothing to Him to find whole towns
in His own Galilee closed against Him by unbelief? to be unable (as the holy record describes it)

to do any mighty work, here, and there, in consequence of their unbelief? to find Jerusalem, the holy
city, locked and barred against its King by fetters
of brass and iron upon the hearts and souls of its
inmates? to die and rise again for man's salvation,
and see thus far but one hundred and twenty
souls plucked out of the national rejection by such
toils, such self-denials, at last such sufferings?
And yet Faith triumphed. He saw by anticipation of the travail of His soul, and was strong to
endure still. He saw the unseen, and He realized
the Invisible.

And Christ conquered Sin by Faith. What
was His temptation but a victory of Faith? the
resolute putting aside of a present gain—let none
deny it, a present good—for the sake of duty,
for the sake of a mission, for the sake of Holy
Scripture and of the will of God? He conquered
sin first in Himself, and then He conquered it
also for His people. And in both cases alike by
faith He conquered.

And Christ conquered Death by Faith. *For
the joy that was set before Him,* writes the
Apostle to the Hebrews, *He endured the Cross.*
He who offers to carry man through death, first

tasted of it for every man. Faith was mighty in Him first of all and prevailed, and then *being made perfect through ·sufferings He became the Author,* to others also, *of eternal salvation.*

Let us bring to Him our own sins to be blotted out, our own sins to be vanquished. Then, living or dying, we are the Lord's. Then in all things —joy or sorrow, sickness or health, hope or fear, life or death—all must be well with us, for *in all these things we are more than conquerors through Him that loved us.*

PRAYER.

For a noble and worthy treatment of this great subject, the reader is referred to a series of Discourses on Prayer in the third volume of the Collected Writings of Edward Irving.

I

PRAYER AN INSTINCT, A MYSTERY, AND A REVELATION.

"Then began men to call upon the name of the Lord."—
GEN. iv. 26.

IKE Faith, like Hope, like Regeneration, like Repentance, like all the mighty workings of the Divine life in man, Prayer also rests, as its indestructible base, upon the accomplished work of our Lord Jesus Christ; even that work of reconciliation in which things in heaven and things on earth, ages past and to come, meet and are at one; that work which made conflict peace, discord harmony, and division unity. That great Easter Day, which brought again from the dead our Lord Jesus—brought Him back as the Mediator and Intercessor and High Priest of man—is the starting-point of Prayer as it is the bulwark of Promise. Whenever therefore we contemplate, with the Church of all time, the sure and certain proofs of Christ's rising; whenever we pass in review the mighty irrefragable evidences which attest to us the certainty, the meaning, and the efficacy of all that was suffered in Gethsemane and on Calvary, and of all that was achieved in the crowning victory of Christ over death and the grave; and whenever we go on to celebrate that other great mystery of Redemption, which is the coming of the Holy Ghost as the Light and Guide and Comforter of God's purchased flock below; then are we laying deep the foundation of doctrine for the belief and the use of that chief ordinary means of communication between the Militant Church on earth and her Divine Life and Head in heaven, which is now to be the subject of our discourse—even the blessed ordinance and institution of which an Apostle wrote, *Pray without ceasing—Praying always with all prayer and supplication in the Spirit, and watching thereunto with all perseverance.*

We will briefly define Prayer, at the outset, as

speaking to God. We will make it embrace more than mere asking. Prayer is not request alone, it is not entreaty alone, it is not intercession alone: still less is it confession or praise or thanksgiving alone : it embraces all. Prayer is not private worship alone, nor domestic, nor social, nor public : it is all. The word is used at present in the widest and most inclusive sense that can be. Prayer is speaking to God—on any subject, with any object, in any place, and in any way.

1. Now the first thought for this time is that Prayer so regarded is an Instinct. It seems to be natural to man to look upwards and to address himself to his God.

All nations have had some power upon which they called in time of need. Some power which they recognized as exercising an influence, malign or benevolent, over individual as well as national destinies. Sometimes—we speak now of heathen nations—the power so invoked was some real property or attribute of the Divine Creator. Some one conception, not untrue but isolated, of the real character of God Himself, was made the whole idea of God and (as such) worshipped. Most often it was mere power;

apart from justice, apart from wisdom, apart from holiness, apart from love. And thus even a real element of God's character may be made into a false deity by being taken alone. In conceiving of God, isolation is distortion—distortion is false-hood—and falsehood is idolatry.

But the point now before us is, that to con-ceive of a Power above, and to turn to that Power in time of need, is one of those natural instincts which God, for our comfort and for our good, has implanted in His rational creatures. The instinct of prayer (like any other instinct) may be abused : the loss of Divine knowledge, whether by the corruption of an original tradition or by the depra-vity of a sensual life, may go so far as to make men think of God as of such an one as themselves ; as of a Being influenced by human motives, of resentment and jealousy, of dislike and partiality, of caprice and desire : or even as of One worse than themselves ; an impersonation of their own evil passions ; all hatred, all cruelty, all suspicion, all lust : and thus religion itself may be turned into a curse and not a blessing, lowering instead of raising the standard of duty, and altogether divorcing the hope of the Divine favour from the endeavour after rectitude or the pursuit of virtue. And yet, even in this depth of lost knowledge and depraved feeling, the instinct of Prayer shall survive and assert itself: a nation going to war with another nation shall call upon its God for success and victory; and an individual man, from the bedside of a dying wife or child, shall invoke the aid of One supposed to be mighty, to stay the course of a disease which the earthly physician has pronounced incurable and mortal.

If this has been true, is true still, in the case of heathen and idolatrous lands, far more true is it where the light of Revelation shines around, though it has not yet touched the individual soul with the rising beam of God's Spirit. We can scarcely perhaps describe as an Instinct, that which brings together on the first day of each week, in every part of Christendom, thousands and tens of thousands of nominal worshippers. It is something more than Instinct, and also it is something less. More, in so far as the worship is occasioned by obedience to an express word of Revelation : less, in so far as the constraining cause of worship is nothing above and nothing within, but only the voice of custom or fashion, of the long use

of ages, or of the vain, thoughtless, frivolous
world.

But although we may not draw our proof from
the mere assembling of ourselves together for the
performance of a too often heartless rite of devotion, we may confidently appeal to the experience
and to the conscience of all, whether there is not
something within us—we can scarcely define or
describe it—which prompts us to make application
to One above in any such emergency as really stirs
the soul's life into an exceptional activity.   The
occasion may be of any kind.   It may be danger.
Not alone in the days of the old Hebrew prophet,
but in all times has it been verified, that, when the
Lord sends a mighty tempest into the sea, the pas-
sengers in their terror cry every man to his God.
Then will men, who, but an hour before, were
heard taking in vain the holy name, or uttering
infidel blasphemies against the blood which bought
them, be heard asking His mercy with importunate
cries, and going down into the deep which is to be
their grave grasping that weapon of All-Prayer at
which till now they have mocked or smiled.   When
the real man is disclosed—for the man seen in common life is commonly not the real man—when the

real man is at last disclosed, there is in him, after all, something which we must describe as an Instinct of Prayer.

And so is it in another kind of danger of which few men have had no experience. It is not only the perils of the sea which bring sin to remembrance. Sometimes the thoughts of the night are troubled and anxious, though the house may be still and secure, and the elements without serene and sleeping. The recollection of a long-neglected duty, or of an oft-committed sin ; the countenance of an injured friend unseen, unthought-of for years, of a parent distressed by ingratitude or neglected in age and loneliness, of a Saviour crucified for us in vain, or a God longsuffering through a lifetime towards a creature unthankful and evil ; such a thought as this, coming we know not whence, has stripped off, as in a moment, a mask of self-excuse and self-deception worn easily and almost naturally in the daylight—revealing a guilt which we cannot gainsay, and prognosticating a future which it is agony to forecast. Who has not felt, in such an experience, the rising cry within, *God be merciful to me a sinner ?* Who has not found that, apart from reasoning or argument on the subject, it was natu-

K

ral to him, at that moment, to seek relief in supplication—to turn, late but eagerly, to a God
neglected yet unforgotten, seeking of Him the
pardon and the cleansing which must be had, and
which cannot elsewhere be hoped for? Just as the
instinct of nature brings the child in distress or
hunger to a father's knee or a mother's bosom,
even so does created man turn in great misery to
a faithful Creator, and, according to his conception
of His attributes and of His workings, throw himself upon His compassion and invoke His aid.
Prayer is an Instinct.

2. But Prayer is a Mystery too.

Some of the commonest of all experiences are
the most mysterious also. What is birth, what is
death—what are sleep and waking—what is habit,
what is influence, what is conscience, what is sin
—what is life itself—but a mystery—a secret un-
told, an enigma inexplicable? Therefore it is no
argument against the truth of any fact, or against
the importance of any duty, that it involves mystery: it is only the more like other certain realities
of man's being, if it involves questions which we
cannot answer, difficulties which we cannot solve.
The instinct of Prayer is a mystery too.

All communications of thought from one mind to another are wonderful. That the utterance of a few sounds, in themselves utterly unmeaning, should enable one man to look into the heart and soul of another; that love and hatred, joy and sorrow, want and satisfaction, should be capable of expressing themselves by those things which we call the gift of speech and the art of language; this is mysterious: in itself, perhaps, scarcely less mysterious than that other processes of communication should be carried on without speech; that the dumb should find means of conveying information by signs, or the absent and distant hold intercourse over sea and land by letters. The wonder may vary with the commonness: but the mystery remains unchanged through all; the mystery of the secret soul making itself, in anẏ way and by any means, intelligible to the mind and heart and spirit of another.

But doubtless there is a mystery in Prayer exceeding and transcending all these. That I by myself, with walls enclosing and doors shut about me, should be able, without speech or sign or letter, by a mere act and effort of will, to convey to One whom I see not, the inmost secrets, the deepest wants, the highest aspirations, the most earnest longings and yearnings, of my spirit ; that I should be able to will my thoughts into another conscious- ness, not by telegraph or magnetism, not by any mechanism of art or man's device, but by the simple thinking of the thought *as if in* that other presence ; that I should be able to carry on whole processes of the most intimate self-explanation, in the confidence that One whom I see not and can- not see reads them with an intuition deeper and more searching than that of the soul which con- ducts them, perceives a depth of meaning which I knew not, and distinguishes, by a discernment beyond mine, between the real and the fancied, between the true and the half-true, whether in the confession or the desire—surely all this is a riddle and a mystery beyond expression or com- prehension ; enough to cause much hesitation and to explain much misgiving in the exercise itself ; enough too, on the other hand, to give strong confirmation to the belief that a practice so deeply rooted in man's habit, being also in itself so beset with intellectual difficulties, must have been im- planted there by Him who made him ; must be, like the bodily appetites, like the natural affections, designed to draw him, as by a gentle compulsion, towards something conducive to his happiness, essential to his good.

And thus the very mysteriousness of Prayer turns into an argument for its reasonableness. It is not a thing which common men would have thought of or gone after for themselves. The idea of holding communication, without speech or sign, with a distant, an unseen, a spiritual Being—of telling wants, anxieties, and sins, of carrying requests and petitions, of offering utterances of praise and thanksgiving, to One of whom the senses take no cognizance and who gives no direct intimation of His presence—is an idea too sublime, too ethereal, for any but poets or philosophers to have dreamed of, had it not been made instinctive by the original Designer of our spiritual frame, for purposes not less necessary, and by a thousand degrees higher and nobler, than the support of the body by its supplies of wholesome food, or the maintenance of society by its bonds of lawful relationship.

3. But we are not left to such inferences of duty, safely and certainly as they might be drawn. The Instinct, and the Mystery, is a Revelation too.

Unfallen man held communion with his Maker.

And though we know not with any exactness the landmarks of fact and of parable in the primeval record; know not for certain how much is history and how much figure in the narrative, for example, which speaks of the Lord God bringing to Adam every living creature, to see what he would call them—or, again, of the Lord God walking in the garden in the cool of the day, and His voice being heard from among the trees of the garden; we must at least gather from such expressions that there was an intercourse and a communication, and that, probably, as indeed we should expect, of a more direct and a more confidential nature than a being spoilt and deformed by sin is at present capable of.

But indeed some communication and intercourse with God remained or was re-instituted after that first transgression. Even Cain, much more Abel, addresses and is answered by the Lord his God. And the dark hint of the text, found at the end of the very chapter which records the first murder, seems to denote some revival and re-establishment, in the form perhaps of ritual and sacrifice, of that open quest and search of God by His sinful children, which is the mark throughout all time, of a Fall unto rising—the promise of a return from wandering, a restoration from exile, a life out of death.

And the very next chapter tells of a saint among the fallen ; of one who upon earth walked with God —how save by Prayer ?—and then was not because God took Him. So that, as we pass on through the pages, now dark now bright, which tell of the chequered lives and varying fortunes of the fallen, who, amidst all their woes and wickednesses, never lost altogether the clue of faith and the prospect of redemption ; we are struck by this, as the one unvarying link between the successive generations of God's children—the possession of an access through prayer to the throne of grace, and of a strength thence derived to fight God's battles and to hand on the torch of God's truth. We see it in Noah, we see it in Abraham, we see it in Joseph, we see it in Moses, we see it in Samuel, we see it in David, we see it in Elijah, we see it along all the line of godly kings, heroic priests, and martyr prophets. Prayer—or (if you go to the root of prayer) faith—this is the common feature which makes God's saints under all Dispensations brethren.

Many things waited for the coming of Christ to reveal them : but Prayer waited not. Piety without knowledge there might be : piety without prayer could not be. And so Christ who came to bring life and immortality to light by His Gospel, had no need to teach as a novelty the duty or the privilege of prayer. He might have much to correct in it, much to elevate, and much to inform : but He was able at least to assume that all pious men, however ignorant, prayed ; and to say therefore only this, *When ye pray, say—After this manner*, not that, *pray ye.*

It was more important still that He Himself should be a Man of Prayer. And O see, ye who call Christ your Example, how He bore Himself towards this duty ! Mark how He linked together two days of toilsome charity by a night of ceaseless Prayer ! Observe how, when He had anything to enjoy, He first looked up to heaven, and remembered God in His gifts ! How, when He had anything to do—whether some choice of representatives, some miraculous cure, some raising from death—He first sought God's converse, God's direction, God's strength, and then did the thing ! *He went out into a mountain and continued all night in prayer to God: and when it was day He called unto Him His disciples, and of them He chose twelve. Looking up to heaven, He sighed, and said unto Him, Ephphatha, that is, Be opened. Father, I thank Thee that Thou hast heard me—Lazarus, come forth!* And how, when He had anything to suffer, He sought through Prayer, as a Man, the courage and the patience. *Being in an agony He prayed* till *the sweat was as it were great drops of blood falling down to the ground. Father, if it be possible, let this cup pass from me. Thy will be done. Father, forgive them, for they know not what they do. Father, into Thy hands I commend my spirit—and when He had said this, He gave up the ghost.*

By the side of this wondrous example, precept itself, even from His lips, falls faint and dead. The Revelation of prayer was in the example. If the Christian life be indeed the imitation of Christ, then must the Christian man be first, and above all else, a man of prayer. Feeling in himself the instinct, while he acknowledges too the mystery, of Prayer, he accepts it also, and before all, as a Revelation, that he who would find God, he who would serve God, he who would hereafter be with God, must first seek Him now by faith, and then after this life have the fruition of His glorious Godhead.

We pause for this time on the very threshold of our great subject, desiring only, and praying, that God of His great mercy will write the word PRAYER upon all our hearts. More and more do we feel that, if a man do but pray, he has entered already upon the way of salvation. It is the test, it is the touchstone, it is the very trial for life and death, of the spiritual life and the eternal hope of every man. And I think too it is one which every man can apply. The man of prayer —yea, the man who prays—knows himself in that character. Yes, I know you would be glad to pray: but as it is, you do not. I know you try to pray: but, as the case now stands, you do not pray. Sometimes you have a feeling that you ought to pray: you rise at midnight and say the words of prayer: but you know that not one echo of your prayer entered heaven. You know that your heart was not there. You know that you addressed no one—and you more than suspect that no one heard! Yes, I know that you felt that that particular sin ought to be mastered; that that difficult, that long-neglected duty ought to be

performed. And you tried to pray for grace to
conquer and do. But when the trial came, you
did not do, and you did not conquer. Look back
from the result to the means—reflect—you never
prayed! Account for it as you may, the heart of
prayer was wanting: there was the form—there
was not the longing will—there was not the fervent desire.

Not to discourage, but to animate—not to daunt
effort, but to stimulate it—do we thus speak. I
know not how it is that there is this difference between man and man: I know not—God knoweth!
But I know this—that the difference lies very high
up; lies in the moving of the will, and not in the
efficacy of the prayer. One man desires to be
holy; desires, and therefore prays. One man is
athirst for God; and therefore comes to Him
who says, *If any man thirst, I will give Him the
water of life freely.* One man hates his sins, and
would give his right hand or his right eye to be
rid of them: and therefore he uses the means;
and when he prays, he means his petition and will
take no denial. And another has but half a heart
after holiness, after piety, after release from sin:
and so, when he asks, he is satisfied with the ask-

ing ; thinks he has done his part, and if the thing asked will not come, he must go without it ! That man does not pray what he himself can call prayer !

The secret is too deep for me : I cannot penetrate it. After all, there is something mysterious in this difference between man and man : shall we ever know what made this man good, and that man bad ? this man earnest and resolute, that man vacillating and half-hearted ? But this, I think, we know already : by what steps we, we ourselves, went down into the faithless, impenitent, prayerless state ; how it came to pass that we—children perhaps of pious parents, nurtured certainly in the same pure Church, knowing the doctrine of god liness, and called again and again by all the promises—yet, ever learning, could never come to the knowledge of the truth ! Yes, we know our own history, though we know not another's : and I think we shall never say, even in the place of torment, that God gave us no chance, or that the fault of our perdition is His !

But O, may He bring us back, while yet there is time, through the gate of penitence into the way of peace—through the prayer of faith into the strength of grace! Not in Him, but in ourselves, are we straitened: not unto ourselves, but unto Him, be the praise of our rescue and of our redemption!

II

PRINCIPLES OF PRAYER.

"I the Lord have spoken it, and I will do it. . . . I will yet for this be enquired of by the house of Israel, to do it for them."—EZEK. xxxvi. 36, 37.

WE have not denied the name of Prayer to any rising of the soul of man towards the Invisible God. It is described by St Paul at Athens as the very end for which God set all nations of men to dwell on all the face of the earth, *that they should seek the Lord, if haply they might feel after Him*— as men grope in the dark or in blindness after some lost or desired thing—*and find* also Him whom they thus feel after, and *in whom*, whether known or unknown, we all *live and move, and have our being.* Even that feeling after God is Prayer.

If it be but the vague cry, sent forth into the infinite void by the hunger or the cold or the nakedness of a spirit created for yet ignorant of its Maker, we have not denied it the name of Prayer: for Prayer is an instinct of nature, as well as a mystery of religion, and a revelation of grace.

But now, in passing on to speak, as God shall enable us, of the Principles of this divine and holy exercise, we must of necessity deal not with the Prayer of Nature, but with the Prayer of the Gospel, which is the Prayer of Faith. It would be a needless and a profitless stepping down from the standing-place which God has given us in His Word and in His Church, to settle how the man ignorant of Revelation, the man with reason only and conscience to enlighten him, should frame that first enquiry by which he is to seek and to feel after a God; what instinctive hopes may animate his search, what rules direct, or what conditions limit it. We speak now as to Christian men, who desire to walk, in this matter as in others, by the light of truth and inspiration, addressing Christ in the soul, as once His disciples said to Him upon earth, in reference to a difficult and an all-important duty—

Lord, teach us to pray.

1. First, then, Prayer is founded upon knowledge.

Prayer, we said, is speaking to God.   Before we can speak to God, we must know God.   *How shall they call,* an Apostle asks, *on Him in whom they have not believed?*   Even the prayer of the heathen, so far as it is prayer, rests upon knowledge.   If he speaks to an idol—if he asks aid of wood or stone, and stops there—then the nonentity of the object communicates itself to the worship : *an idol is nothing in the world,* and the prayer which treats it as an existence is itself a nothingness too.   But if the heathen man in any degree looks through the idol to a Being conceived of as distinct from it ; if he so much as recognizes one of God's real attributes, say even power, and addresses himself to that ; then, in the same proportion, the lie of his idolatry becomes tinged and tinctured with a truth, and the cry, *O Baal, hear us,* may be the faint shadow and reflection of a better worship, because it also, even it, has this characteristic of the Prayer we speak of, that it is founded (in some one point at least) upon knowledge. The man has an idea of God as a God of power. The prayer which knew nothing whatever of its object, or which called upon Him in no one respect as He is, would lack the first principle of all prayer, that it must have a basis of knowledge.

And are no Christian prayers—are no prayers, I mean, of Christians so called—utterly destitute of this first condition?

To how many might the remonstrance of God now be addressed, *Thou thoughtest wickedly that I am even such an one as thyself;* such in discernment, such in equity, such in veracity, or such in power! How many, even in prayer, never let God into their secrets; hope to elude His inspection, try to baffle His intuition! How many, even in prayer, expect of God a treatment neither just nor moral; ask of Him some compromise with evil, and a salvation not from but in their sins! How many, even in prayer, act the hypocrite and the dissembler; professing desires which they feel not, and regrets and repentances which deceive not even themselves! How many still expect to be heard for their much speaking, or to overbear the counsels of the Unchangeable by the vehemence of their importunity! All such prayers lack the first

L

requisite—the knowledge, the true knowledge, of Him to whom they are offered.

Let the man who would pray aright begin by studying his Bible. Let him first acquaint himself with God, and then speak to Him. The Word of God tells us in a thousand manners what He is in Himself, and what He is in His doings towards the children of men. Sometimes by precept, sometimes by warning; sometimes by example, sometimes by judgment; sometimes by a record of praise, and sometimes by an interposition of punishment; always by the exhibition of a perfect insight, an exact discernment, an earnest approbation of good and an absolute abhorrence of evil; the Bible makes known to us in every possible aspect the character and mind of its Author; does for us what no intimacy of conversation and no frequency of correspondence, together, can ever do for us in the case of a man; inasmuch as here alone is no possibility of variableness, of change, of surprise, or caprice; here alone is a Spirit and a Life the same yesterday and to-day and for ever —as independent of interference from without, as of disturbance within—as Omnipotent and Omnipresent to execute, as Omniscient to discover, All-wise to resolve, All-just to judge, and All-merciful to save. He who would ask of God must first know God; and he must carry that knowledge into the asking. He must never ask of God anything which it would contradict the character of God to grant. He must never ask the All-holy to miscall an act, nor the All-true to misread a motive. He must never so press upon one attribute as to force it into collision and conflict with another. He must not, because God is merciful, ask Him to be unjust; nor, because God is patient, ask Him to forego judgment. The prayer which presupposes knowledge must also be a prayer which recognizes and remembers it.

And when we speak of knowledge, let us not lose ourselves in vague generalities—or in the discussion of God's qualities and properties and attributes—without remembering first how God has illustrated, and then how God has embodied for us the revelation of Himself.

Faint and poor were terms like power and justice and righteousness—phrases like goodness, or mercy, or even love itself—to convey to our dark minds and cold hearts the requisite acquaintance with God. It pleased Him therefore to describe

Himself to us under figures of human trust and relationship; calling Himself our Lord, our Ruler, our King—our Guide, our Protector, our Shepherd, our Friend—at last our Father; thus teaching us to pass through all abstractions of quality, disposition, or virtue, into the conception of a living Person, concerned in us and occupied about us, One in whom the life may find strength and the soul repose.

Yet even these figures of office and relationship towards us might fail, might perplex, might even mislead. If man took but one of them, he might limit the idea of God still: if he took one of them with another, he might still blur, confuse, or distort the image. The King might be all sternness: the Friend might be all indulgence: even the Father might be too entirely authority, or too entirely affection. How then could God, seeking to combine and harmonize man's knowledge, set His opposite perfections at one, and enable the creature who would worship Him aright to approach Him not as this alone or that, but as all that He is, and is for Him? Blessed be God, we know the answer. *No man hath seen God at any time:* even His revelations of Himself, read in a book, could but faintly disclose Him : *the only be-gotten Son, which is in the bosom of the Father, He hath declared Him.* *He that hath seen me,* He said Himself, *hath seen the Father : and how sayest thou then, Show us the Father ?* In Christ we see God not only as that which He is, but as all that He is : not only as powerful, or only as just, or only as wise, or only as good—but as all : not only as a Ruler, or only as a Protector, or only as a Friend —but as all : not only in feeling, or only in will, or only in action—but in all these ; combining hatred against sin with tenderness towards the sinner, perfect truth with absolute love, the cancelling of guilt by a free forgiveness, with the executing judg-ment upon all corruptions both in the severities of a suffering life and in the slow and difficult sanctification of a sin-stained and sin-damaged soul.

In Christ God is revealed : and upon the know-ledge of Christ, therefore, is prayer to God founded. The words with which Christian supplication is always winged and speeded—*through Jesus Christ our Lord—through Jesus Christ our only Mediator and Advocate—through the merits of our only Lord and Saviour Jesus Christ*—are a perpetual memento of that first condition of Prayer, on which we are dwelling, that it be founded on the true knowledge of God, and carry that knowledge with it to the mercy-seat of God's presence.

Remember also that the knowledge of God in Christ is of necessity a self-knowledge also. It is when the sinner can say, *I have heard of Thee with the hearing of the ear, but now mine eye seeth Thee;* that he can add, for the first time it may be, with perfect intelligence, *Wherefore I abhor myself, and repent in dust and ashes.* He who knows God in Christ, knows himself also. Then first he discovers what sin is, and what his own share in it; the one how black and hateful, the other how deep and large: he who comes thus to God, comes neither veiled nor boastful; comes as a sinner indeed to One who nevertheless in Christ Jesus is both his Father and his God still.

2. Secondly, Prayer founded on knowledge is prompted by desire. The man who asks of God must desire too.

This might seem to be evident. It is an unmeaning form—in human intercourse it would be felt as an insult—to ask for that which we desire not.

But let a man examine himself, and how will he find it to be in things Divine?

Look at the history of your prayers. Did not the rule and custom of praying precede, in point of time, the rise in you of spiritual desire? Where is that form of words for the prayer of a child, which has nothing in it but what a child can wish for?

Or look at the experience—the later, I might say the present, experience—of your own prayers. Who has not some words of course—some constant, unvaried expressions of request — which recur, even in private, when he kneels to pray? some phrases, brief, it may be, and simple, without which he scarcely feels that his prayer would be prayer at all? And yet how often is that man's soul out of tune even for this most indispensable, perhaps this most elementary, petition! How often does the prayer for pardon come from one who is neither grieved nor burdened with his guilt, and the prayer for grace and sanctification from one who has every expectation, if not every intention, of continuing in sin!

And if this last is a supposition (as God grant it may be) repudiated by a large part of the Christian congregation as too dark a picture to represent them;

let me at least speak of our public worship, and notice how many of our Church prayers, offered day by day or week by week in the House of God, are beside the mark of universal desire on the part of those who offer them. If at the close of any service you were asked to open your Book of Prayer, and, turning back to the Office of Worship just ended, to point to those particular Collects, those requests, those intercessions, which had expressed, in the ear of God, your own honest, hearty, earnest desires, and which had had therefore for you, on that one occasion at least, this second condition of all Prayer, that it be prompted by desire; how much of the whole service would appear, by this test, to have been, on your part, prayer at all? That only have you indeed prayed, which you indeed desired. How much was this?

It will be said indeed, and most truly, that spiritual desires are of tardy if not late growth in any man; and that being like almost all that is in us, whether of good or evil, of the nature (when they are formed) of habits, it is needful that they be fostered in us by use, practice, and exercise. Things which the child desires not, by reason of inexperience and ignorance, the man may come to desire by the help of pious custom and habitual devotion. Besides which, Prayer is not only the expression of desire, but in great part also an act of obedience. We must begin by obeying. The Lord's Prayer itself, taught us by Christ as a specimen and summary of all Prayer, and used by Christian people as an act of duty and reverence towards their Master, has in it much that is difficult; much that rises above the level of the natural or even of the instructed man's wishes: even that must be postponed or discarded, if nothing is of the nature of Prayer, which is not also wrung from our lips by the urgency of present desire.

Thus we enter upon some of the difficult questions which attend the work of our education, in youth or age, for heaven. How early is it wise to bring a child into the congregation, knowing that that child's utterances, whether of prayer or praise, of confession or thanksgiving, must be of necessity everywhere inadequate, in many parts ignorant? How far is it right to maintain, in private or in public, habits of prayer which have ceased to be in harmony with the habits of the life ? How long ought a man to go on praying when it is evident that he has no care to leave off sinning ? And in cases not of utterly careless and by no means of immoral living, what rule shall be laid down for the utterance or the omission, in our prayers, of those requests which ought to be, which sometimes are, but which are not at this moment, desires also of the heart ?

These questions belong not to this time. But it may have served, nevertheless—God grant it—a useful purpose, with a view to our own correction and advancement in godliness, to have thus laid down once again to ourselves this plain principle— that nothing has at any time the characteristics of Prayer, which is not desired; that, if we would pray for forgiveness, we must desire forgiveness; if we would pray for the Holy Spirit, we must desire the Holy Spirit, inasmuch as Prayer is the expression not of a want only but of a wish too, and he only can ask of God who has felt himself in the particular instance to be destitute and needy and unhappy without Him.

3. Prayer, founded on knowledge, and prompted by desire, must, in the third and last place, be bounded by promise.

Not every desire is a fit subject for prayer. No one would pray a sinful wish: there are desires which, like birds of evil omen, shun, of themselves, the light of God. This strong example shows that there is a limit to prayer even within the province of desire: a prayer might be sincere, in so far as it breathed a wish, and yet conscience itself might condemn it as unfit for God's hearing.

When we pursue and ponder this distinction—and it is an important one—we shall find no rest for our reflections till we reach this point—that Promise is the chart and rudder and compass of supplication; that only such things as God has promised are safe and fitting topics for His people's prayers.

We are not counselling that poor and servile use of the word of promise, which would turn the texts of the Bible into a string of engagements and compacts, which are to be urged as it were and pleaded, singly and severally, as making God man's debtor, and false if He pays not. The Bible is not thus indexed and labelled for quotation, nor is the free Spirit thus to be tied and fettered by the lifeless letter. Away with such uses of the Bible as would make it over again a mere Decalogue of conditions and precepts, instead of a fresh rustling breeze, sweeping with health and fragrance over the dry arid wastes of man's servitude and man's corruption.

Nevertheless the manner of God's dealing is largely by promise, and on the ground of that promise must we deal with Him. From the beginning it has been so. God's covenant has been evermore a covenant of promise. Not a contract or compact ; not, Bring this, and I will accept ; not, Do this, and I will bless : but rather, *I promise, therefore live—I promise, therefore love !* The covenant itself was promise. And that Prayer which is based on knowledge must ever on that account be based on promise.

The promise of which we speak is no single separate utterance ; no number, no multitude, of bare literal engagements, which must be found somewhere in the bond, and then rehearsed, by page and clause, as the justification of the particular demand. The promise of God, like the revelation of God, like the counsel of God, like the character of God, is at once ample to magnificence and simple even to unity. One broad, deep, majestic stream, like the river which went forth from Eden, compasses all God's earth, and waters on every side the garden of His creation.

It is the declaration of His will that all should be saved. It is the cry from the temple-court on the last and great day of the feast, *If any man thirst, let him come unto me and drink. There is a river, the streams whereof shall make glad the city of God, the holy place of the tabernacles of the Most High. God is in the midst of her, she shall not be moved: God shall help her, and that right early. This is the will of God, even your sanctification.*

This is the will of God, even your salvation.

So then, whatsoever thing, small or great as man judges—for in God's sight all things are equal—whatsoever thing, inward or outward, in providence or in grace, can promote in any manner the present or the ultimate welfare of one for whom Christ died—that is a fitting subject for prayer, for that lies within the ample region of the promise. Whether it be the giving of some good thing, or the averting of an evil; whether it be the putting away by absolution of an accusing past, or the brightening into comfort of a threatening future; whether it be the strengthening of the human weakness for conflict, or the assurance of the Divine love for peace; whether it be the removal of some cup of sorrow, or the transformation of some cross into a grace,

or the refreshing of the soul by some particular
ordinance of communion, or the gradual putting
down of rebel hosts within, or the sure and conscious ripening of the whole man for glory—all
these are yours as lawful topics of supplication,
for all these are yours as express items of promise.

And what then is excluded? What mean the
words, *Prayer bounded by promise?* Might we
not rather say, Prayer extended, expanded, eman-
cipated, by promise? For where is that circumstance of life, however grievous—where is that
trial or that bereavement, that infirmity or that
temptation, that misgiving or that anguish—which
does not fall within the scope of God's promise,
*All things shall work together for good—Call upon
me in the time of trouble: so will I hear thee, and thou
shalt praise me?*

There is no limit to prayer, but promise; and
no limit to promise, but the soul's good. If we so
pray as to forget that, then we overstep. Then
indeed, no promise being with us, but the reverse
of promise, we pray presumptuously, and mercy
herself shall stop the ear. Seeking great things
for ourselves in this life, pleasures, riches, honours
—exemption from earth's cares, all sunshine, no

cloud nor rain nor storm below—the prayer shall miss its aim, because the prayer has divorced itself from the promise. Happy he, who, so pray-ing, is answered by contraries! Happy he, who, asking health, gains sickness—praying for success and honour, receives instead disappointment and obscurity. This is because the great promise over-shadows him still : because He who loves him will not let him go ; will seek him and win him and save him still, and even because He loves, must refuse!

Prayer is bounded by promise. What God pro-mises not, ask not. What falls not within the scope of the great promise, could not benefit : ask it not. If God gives such a thing, He gives it of spontan-eous love ; gives it because He first makes it safe ; gives it because He would draw forth praise, and show that He has pleasure in the prosperity of His servant.

Prayer bounded by promise turns into an argu-ment for prayer a thought which is sometimes used against it. Men say, How can you hope to change the mind of God by your asking? *I am the Lord : I change not.* It is presumptuous in the creature to expect to alter in any point the pur-. pose of the Creator. Answer, It is because God is

unchangeable that I pray.   The unchangeableness
of God must extend surely to His promise.   If
He has affixed, of His own will, His giving to
man's asking; if He has said, *Ask, and ye shall
have;* if He has said, *Whatsoever ye shall ask
in prayer, believing, ye shall receive;* the very im-
mutability of His counsel is my plea for praying.
If God changes not, neither does God's promise.
Hath He said, and shall He not do it?   That
which you claim for God's will, I claim for God's
word—namely, that in it *there is no variableness
neither shadow of turning.*   And although I see not
as yet fully, I can already see in part, that it is
of wisdom, and that it is for His glory, to wed
prayer to promise.   *I the Lord have spoken it*, is
the memorable record before us, *and I will do it:
yet for this will I be enquired of by you.*   The
promise itself waits prayer for its fulfilment.   God
will do it: but God must be enquired of still.
Thus He makes man know who gives.   Thus He
prompts search after Him whom to know is eternal
life.   Thus He brings man near to Himself, and
keeps him—blessed above all blessing—where, in
His presence, is fulness of joy, where, at His right
hand, there are pleasures for evermore.

III

HINDRANCES AND AIDS TO PRAYER.

"Then I said, I am cast out of Thy sight: yet I will look
again toward Thy holy temple."—JONAH ii. 4.

THE work of Prayer is not easy. It
cannot be so. To communicate with
another world—to call upon an un-
seen Person—to ask for that which is spiritual
—to acknowledge a power out of ourselves
as working for us, and to ask that that power
should so work for us as to lead, by a path
which Nature likes not, to a destination which
Nature desires not—all this is full of difficulty.
The hindrances to such an act of the soul must
be many: if we would ever perform it, God must
help.

That is our subject. Prayer in its Hindrances:
Prayer in its Aids.

M

And let us not look at this subject in a dry abstract way, as though it concerned not us, the very souls and spirits here lying *naked and opened* before Him to whom in a few short years we must all give account ; but rather so speak and so hear as if it were to each one, as indeed it is, a question of life unto life, or else (which God forbid) of death unto death.

When two near friends meet each other, and conversation flags and droops between them—or when two near friends are severed by circumstances, and letters become by degrees few or cold or scanty, so that months and years pass without one unbosoming of the soul, or one living interchange of thought and interest—how is it to be accounted for ? The fault may lie here or there —there may be faults (as we say) on both sides— but the explanation on either side will always be this—there is a suspicion of change in him, or else a reality of change in me. I fancy him altered to me, or I am altered towards him. I have listened perhaps to some mischievous and probably false rumour, of slighting or unfriendly words concerning me, or else of deterioration and degeneracy in

him.   Or I have inferred a change towards me from
a want of regularity or frequency, whether of correspondence or intercourse, for which I myself am
at least equally to blame.   More probably I myself am changed towards him : new friends have
supplanted the old, or the current of feeling has
altered with changes of circumstance, and I neither
give him the affection of the past, nor care for the
former love from him.

Even thus is it—with reverence be it spoken—
when there is an interruption of intercourse between a man and his God.

We might enumerate a multitude of causes,
but if we sought to trace them up to their source
and spring, there could be but two : an erro-
neous idea of God, or else a wrong feeling to
wards Him.

Prayer is founded on knowledge, and Prayer is
prompted by desire.   If then for knowledge there
be error, and if instead of desire there be coldness,
then is Prayer hindered.

Let us look into these two hindrances sepa-
rately.

1. It cannot be denied that we are all prone to

error as to God's character and as to His mind towards us.

Many of us conceive of God Himself in an unlovely aspect.

Sometimes we misinterpret the figures by which God's Word describes Him. When we read of Him as feeling anger, hatred, jealousy ; as executing vengeance upon enemies who yet are also His creatures ; it is not given to every man to see that He is speaking after the manner of men—attributing to Himself motives which would in human beings account for such or such actions, rather than indicating those motives which do in fact influence His own procedure.

And so when God's Word speaks of Him as altering His procedure under the influence of human conduct—repenting, for example, of the evil which He had thought to do, or repenting of some great work of His own because of the iniquity of man—as though things came to Him by surprise, and otherwise than as He had expected or calculated ; these expressions too are capable of an interpretation disparaging and injurious ; taking them servilely and by the letter, we lower, through them, instead of raising, our conception of God.

Thus too there are passages which speak of God's sovereignty in terms which, over-pressed, or taken alone, might seem to imply something arbitrary in Him or even capricious. As when St Paul, quoting a text of the Old Testament concerning king Pharaoh, closes his argument with these words, *Therefore hath He mercy on whom He will have mercy, and whom He will He hardeneth.* Take that verse away from its context; sever it from other sayings which tell of God's bounty in giving, and of God's righteousness in judging; argue from it as if it stood alone in the Bible as a description of God's character and of God's dealing; and how easily might you distort it into a reason for reckless living—for restraining prayer and renouncing effort! If God wills to save, He saves; saves in the midst of careless, prayerless, prodigal riot; saves by spontaneous grace, saves by irresistible power. I may go where I will, and do what I will, till the call comes : and then, without my will, or even against my will, I shall find myself overpowered with a free salvation. And if God wills not to save, then He saves not : no resolutions, no efforts, no tears, no prayers, can draw down upon the desiring soul His answer of peace.

Whom He will He hardeneth. Such readings of God's Word have been made an excuse, by some, for a life of profligacy: in the hands of false or random teachers, they have made sad the hearts of men, daunting the very endeavour after godliness, or even repelling them from such a God as this fearful heresy painted.

So is it, once again, with that perversion and profanation of the true Gospel, which represents the Father as all wrath, and the Son as all charity; paints God armed with the thunderbolt, and the Son interposing between it and its object. Trinitarianism itself, the faith of the Christian, is often Tritheism in disguise: God the sinner's dread, and Christ the sinner's hope. When shall we learn the true revelation, as St John, as St Peter, as St Paul, has described it— God loving the world, and therefore Christ dying —God out of marvellous love sending Christ, and Christ performing the Father's will in dying for the sins of a world?

These are examples of perversions of doctrine as to the character of God. Equally dangerous are those which misrepresent His feeling towards us. As the former set Him in an unlovely, so do these place Him in an unloving light.

Wrong inferences have been drawn by some from the experience of the personal life.

If God loved me—some men say—could He have made me thus? Could He so have consti-tuted my bodily frame, as that every nerve is a torment? or my mental frame, as that every com-panionship is an irritation? or my spiritual frame, as that every duty is a burden, and all devotion a weariness? Why is my earthly life all trial, and my soul's life all gloom? How can I approach with delight a Creator who has thus made, or a Master who would thus reap where He has not sown? How it may be with others, I know not: for myself, I can but lie still, rather sullen than submissive, under the mighty hand of God—not that He may exalt me in due time, but that at last He may have taken His fill in punishing.

Or, once again, we may misplace the declara-tions of God's displeasure against sin. We may fancy Him unwilling to listen to us because of our transgressions. We may shrink from Him because we imagine that He must shrink from us. That displeasure which is really against our wicked-

nesses, we often think of as turned against ourselves.   And thus the plainest assurances of His
readiness, of His desire, to receive us back—to
forgive us the past, and wash us from our defile-
ments — may be rendered inaudible and unper-
suasive to us, because of an idea, drawn too
correctly from human experience, that God is
alienated by reason of sin from the voice and from
the person of the sinner.

2. Thus a wrong idea of God—of His character
as unlovely, or of His mind as unloving towards
us—is one chief impediment to the work of prayer.
The other is, a wrong feeling towards Him.   Not
misconception, not error, but (in the plainest
sense of the words) some form or other of sin.

How close is the connection between a sinful
and a prayerless life !

You may apply to your own life, with confidence,
the criterion and touchstone of Prayer.

Can you pray, with readiness and comfort?   Can
you begin the day with earnest, calm, confiding
prayer?   Can you end the day with quiet, peaceful, filial prayer?   And that, not in a few vague,
unmeaning, unmeant words, but in the fulness of a
self-abasing God-adoring supplication?   Then is

there nothing (as we say) upon your mind; nothing burdening the conscience, nothing staining the life. You have need indeed just to wash the feet—soiled with earth's contact, and wearied with the travail and turmoil of earth's passing day—but having done so, you are clean every whit: you go forth to the day's toil, the Lord sustaining you: you lie down in peace and take your rest, the Lord watching over you, neither slumbering nor sleeping.

But do you find that you cannot pray? Do you find, when you kneel on your knees at morning, something rising within, as it were to choke your utterance? Do you hear, within, a sort of mocking echo, saying, How canst thou ask this of God, thou who desirest not the thing asked! thou who didst yesterday, and (opportunity being given) wilt certainly do to-day, the very thing prayed against? And at evening, the same voice, upbraiding or taunting, with the question, How canst thou say thou art sorry for this thing, which was no surprise and no novelty; which thou hast done often beforetime, and (life being prolonged) wilt certainly do often again? Then indeed is it time that we should stand still and reckon with ourselves carefully, if so be we may yet lay aside this weight which hangs upon us, and get rid of the sin which thus easily and thus pertinaciously besets.

We have spoken as if the sin were one of act and evil habit; a sin to which conscience cannot be blind, nor, seeing it, insensible. But St Peter bids us extend the same thought to transgressions far less palpable. Even family bickerings—even the little daily misunderstandings which arise so readily among members of one household—even the want of due *honour to the weaker vessel,* itself too *heir* with us *of the grace of life*—he bids us beware of, for the same reason—*that your prayers be not hindered.* There must be peace at home, if there is to be intercourse with God.

And indeed it is wonderful how sensitive is that balance to which we are here bringing the condition, as toward God, of the spirit which is in us. Apart from any outward manifestation, whether in act or word, of the evil lurking within, it is enough that it be—that it so much as exist in the deep of the heart—to prevent and stifle prayer. One unlawful wish cherished, one hankering after the forbidden thing allowed in us, one longing look fixed upon the tree of the knowledge of evil—even if there be neither the act nor so much as the purpose of gratification—is enough to keep man from the mercy-seat, and make him tremble at the voice, before familiar, of the Lord his God. It may even be, that the wish is more than the act. An unstable soul may be lured unawares into transgression ; and there may be even less there of guilt than in the heart which ponders, lusts, but does not. To *take pleasure in,* is a later stage of corruption, St Paul tells us, than even to *do.*

And we must go further still, and speak not only of acts, and not only of desires, of evil, as impediments to Prayer, but also of omissions of duty, whether it be toward God or toward man. The consciousness of one known but un-done duty is enough to draw a curtain between the soul and God. Many men are kept from Prayer by neglecting Communion. Many by neglecting the Bible. Many by hardness in com-passionating, and niggardliness in giving. Many by the knowledge that they are unkind to their own flesh and blood ; contented to let others want or be desolate, may they but themselves either keep or else squander !

So then, pursuing this enquiry through the lurk-ing places of the life and of the heart, we shall find this, I doubt not, the most fruitful and the least ambiguous cause of the unwelcomeness and irksomeness of prayer, that, though we know God, we yet glorify Him not as God ; take not His will for our guide, nor His Spirit for our strength ; but walk, in one respect or in many, in the way of our own hearts, and *turn away from Him who speaketh from heaven.*

Thus, the second part of our subject springs naturally from the first. The helps will be, in each point, the converse and opposite of the hindrances. Whatever makes us know God better, and whatever makes us love God more, will be an aid and help to prayer.

Acquaint now thyself with Him, and be at peace.

It is one chief office of the Bible, to assist Prayer by revealing God. Day by day we ought to read, mark, and digest God's holy Word ; saying as we begin, Lord, open Thou mine eyes that I may see Thee in it ; that I may know Thee by the help of it, and so be drawn towards Thee, in reverent worship, as the alone Author and Giver of every good thing. And in proportion as we read with this purpose, we shall profit by and we shall

love the Bible. Look upon it as you would upon
a letter from a distant friend; a transcript of his
present mind, a communication of his wishes and
of his feelings towards you. Look upon it as you
look upon visiting one who is to you as your own
soul; an opportunity of increased knowledge,
which increase of knowledge is evermore also an
increase of love. Then shall we hear no more the
confession of weariness in the study of the Bible :
we shall have turned it to its true account, and be
able at last to say with the Psalmist, *Lord, how I
love Thy Word: all the day long is my study in it.*

Thus will it be also with the hearing of the
Word in public. *Praying's the end of preaching.*
If preaching be what it ought to be, it is the un-
folding, in some definite point, from the sure record
of Inspiration, of the mind of God; the showing
forth of what He is, in counsel and in operation ;
that so the hearts of the hearers may be drawn to
Him (under grace) with a more earnest longing
and a more entire devotion. The value of each
particular Sermon may be estimated, not by the
beauty of its language, and not by the power of its
argument, but by this question rather, Did it make
me pray? Did it send me home with a more in-

telligent mind as to what God is, and a more glow-
ing desire to go to Him and to abide with Him?

Another of the aids to Prayer is what we term
comprehensively the discipline of life.   God has
other modes of instruction concerning Himself,
besides the Word read and the Word preached.
And these other modes of instruction (could we
but accept them) have the same end in view; the
drawing forth into communication with Himself, of
the minds and souls of His creatures.   Even the
severer and sterner of His dealings have this end.
Even the cares and losses, even the trials and sorrows, even the disasters and the desolations.   Use
them thus—treat them as friends in disguise—regard
them not as lashes and scourges, but as calls and
invitations from God—and they too shall have lost
their sting.   Receive them as proofs of His will
that you should be saved, of His desire that you
should die happy; make them, in short, not hindrances but aids to prayer; and you will bless
God for them through the endless age!   How
much more easily should we see this purpose of
love in dispensations not grievous; in the patient
continuance to us, through long years of sin and of
provocation, of all God's common gifts, of life and

reason, of food and raiment, of light and sunshine and fruitful seasons; in the occasional gleams which shoot across the darkest existence, of comfort and hope, of relief and peace! These, even more readily than the opposite, should be aids and helps to prayer: for their very tone is persuasion, their very voice is love.

Finally, we may encourage ourselves with this recollection, that the chiefest of the helps to Prayer is Prayer. Pray once, and you will pray again. Pray as you can to-day—and to-morrow you shall pray better. If you wait to pray till prayer shall be less difficult, you will never pray. The voice of God is calling to you, *Seek ye my face:* it is your duty, it is your happiness, it is your life: that voice calls to you in many ways, calls in Scripture, calls from this Pulpit, calls in Conscience, calls in Providence, calls in every event, common or special, glad or grave, welcome or sorrowful: see that, when God says, *Seek ye my face*, we be ready, every one to answer with the Psalmist, *Thy face, Lord, will I seek!* Answer thus, and each day shall make the reply heartier and more spontaneous. It is by honestly trying to pray, that we can alone learn to pray. No elaborate treatises, no exhaustive Sermons, laying down the rules or enforcing the arguments for prayer, will avail anything, so long as the knee actually bends not and the soul itself speaks not in God's presence. Then the first step is indeed taken: and that first step is a step towards heaven. Then is the barrier broken down, and the *great gulf fixed* bridged over. *Then shall we know, if we follow on to know the Lord.* Then shall the experience of life enforce and explain within us the record of Revelation, and God Himself in both shall be the Teacher. Then, as days pass by, and we grasp the living clue to the labyrinth of being, in the purpose of God Himself to save our souls, we shall find the effort changed into the reality, and the habit into the necessity, of Prayer : we shall be as little able to dispense with Prayer as with food, as thankful for the bread from heaven as dependent for daily life upon the bread of earth. And when on any particular day the spring of Prayer seems for the moment dry or sealed within ; when we kneel without desire, say the words without feeling them, and ask for that which we ought to hunger after yet hunger not ; then shall we gather both hope and also wisdom from prolonged experience : we shall take the key of intercession, or the key of thanksgiving, or the key of simple adoration, to unlock the chamber of personal petition ; and find once again, as we have found often before, that the Lord's arm is not shortened, nor His ear heavy; that the promise to all is a promise also to each ; and that blessed is he, and he only, who can echo from his heart the memorable resolution, *One thing have I desired of the Lord, that will I seek after ; that I may dwell in the house of the Lord all the days of my life, to behold the beauty of the Lord, and to enquire in His temple.*

IV

PRAYER IN ITS RELATION TO ACTION.

" Then flew one of the Seraphims unto me, having a live
   coal in his hand, which he had taken with the tongs
   from off the altar.

And he laid it upon my mouth, and said, Lo, this hath
   touched thy lips ; and thine iniquity is taken away, and
   thy sins purged.

Also I heard the voice of the Lord, saying, Whom shall I
   send, and who will go for us?   Then said I, Here am I ;
   send me."—Isa. vi. 6-8.

THERE is an inward life in every man,
and an outward. A secret life, which
he lives in himself and before his God ;
with which a stranger intermeddles not, and in
which, for good or evil, he is all alone. And a
visible life, which he lives in work and speech, in
business and society ; influencing and being influenced, for good or evil ; serving or else neglecting

his own one generation, and in it glorifying or else dishonouring the God who made and the Lord who bought him.

Now there must of necessity be a connection and a reciprocity between these two. The inward life and the outward must affect and be affected by each other. No man can erect a barrier for himself between the secret self and the visible; or say, What I am towards God is one thing, and what I am before man is another thing, and the two things shall have no community of being, and no mutual influence. The inward life must tell upon the outward, and the visible man affect and react upon the secret.

To express the matter in the terms of our present subject, there must be a relation between Prayer and Action; between Prayer, which is the soul of the inward life, and Action, which is the substance of the outward.

But, though the two lives cannot be entirely divorced, they are seldom absolutely united. The inward life and the outward are seldom equally developed. In most men there is a disproportion —in some, a vast disproportion—between the activity of the soul and the activity of the life.

There is a relation, but it is an unequal and a distorted relation, between the inward man and the outward. It is possible for a life of action to be a life without prayer. And it is possible— though the experience is less common—for a life of prayer to be a life of no activity.

Look for a moment at the two phenomena. It will help the understanding of what follows, thus to separate the two ideas, Prayer, and Action.

We have called Prayer an instinct. It is natural, we believe, to man to look upward, and to call in God. In distress and danger, in the great anxieties and terrible crises of human exist- ence, even the infidel, even the scoffer, will pray. But since Prayer is not an instinct only, but a mystery too ; an idea as difficult to grasp as im- possible to explain ; an exercise demanding time, and effort, and abstraction of thought, and prepara- tion of heart ; a work, moreover, which is over- looked by no taskmaster, and sanctioned by no immediate or definite penalty ; it is not to be won- dered at if it is often put aside ; if men of business fill their day with what is (in a worldly sense) necessary, and drive Prayer into corners; or if, in the end, Prayer slips altogether out of the common life; put off till some *convenient season* of leisure or of emergency, when it may come back of itself and be found instantly possible and certainly comforting! It is thus, doubtless, God being the witness, in ten thousand times ten thousand human lives. What remains of Prayer is as good as nothing: it is not Prayer. It is but some relic of a long-past infancy, by which we would hold on, as it were, to a faith which we may one day want, and which meanwhile we would not violently outrage. It is no part of the life: it could be flung away to-morrow, no man missing it: it is disconnected utterly from the life which is real and from the interests which are essential. Prayer and Action have parted company: the outward life has swallowed up the inward, and the shrine of God's worship has become the money-changer's counting-house. When God is called in, it will be a signal of disappointment and discomfiture; of the wreck of a life's ventures, and the palsy of a life's energies. And meanwhile Action seems oftentimes to prosper wonderfully without Prayer. The hand is as steady, the step as firm—the calculation as exact, the reasoning as logical—strange to say, the conduct as respectable, and the home as peaceful—as if

God were in all the thoughts! *Lo, these are the ungodly; these prosper in the world, and these have riches in possession. They are not in trouble,* the Psalmist says, *as other men. There are no bands even in their death.* It was a perplexity and a stumblingblock to him. He began to say, *I have cleansed my heart in vain, and washed my hands in innocency. All the day long have I been punished, and chastened every morning.* But at last he *went into the sanctuary of God,* and there he *understood the end of these men :* he saw what becomes at last of Action without Prayer—how it is *brought into desolation as in a moment,* when God *makes its image to vanish out of His city !*

It is less needful to dwell upon the opposite thought, of a life of Prayer divorced from Action, because it is not the error of our times; in which religion itself runs commonly to an upward and an outward growth, and too often has no root in the deep rich soil of a soul's communion with God. But this thing also has been, may be, and sometimes is. Here the one thought is, the study of heaven, the meditation of eternity; the constant realization of things unseen, the undisturbed anticipation of things hoped for; the culture of the individual soul for God's presence, the preparation of the individual being for the inheritance of the saints in light. Such was the aim of those monastic institutions, which sheltered many a timid or penitent soul from shocks or wiles of temptation to which the courage of faith was unequal; nursed (we cannot doubt) many a saint for glory, in a seclusion scarcely more repulsive to nature than spiritually luxurious; yet were diametrically opposed to the first principle of the Gospel, which would have men to be in the world, though not of it; working for God, and witnessing for God, and representing God, amidst their fellows; showing what the strength of grace is, the power of meekness, the force of holiness, the energy of consistency, the might of love; in short, letting the Gospel light so shine before men, that they, seeing it in that reflection, may be brought to glorify with them a Father in heaven. Where the one object is made to be the safety of the individual soul, there can at least be no *holding forth*, no presentation, that is, to others, of *the word of life:* the flame may burn for a while under its bushel, but it can have no catching and kindling vigour in a world lying around it in wickedness. The same error is seen, and in a less excusable form, in many modern systems of Christian doctrine; in which an arbitrary distinction is drawn between the Church and the world, and a large part of religious duty is made to consist in shutting up and isolating the sympathies and energies of the Divine life; confining them within the limits of the society of the like-minded, and counting as a dangerous licence any attempt at communication or communion with those who speak not the self-same word and mete not with the very same measure in the discrimination of things that differ. Christ knows not of a Church within the Church: He would have the example and the influence of His saints diffused, generously and equally, amongst the great congregation of His redeemed.

We have taken two examples; the extremes of distance and difference between the life of Action and the life of Prayer. But speaking on the Lord's Day in the Lord's House, we do well to remember that it is in the debatable ground between these two that the bulk of our hearers, and therefore the staple of our exhortations, must find their place. An utter neglect of Prayer can scarcely be imputed to those who are here gathered to worship. And an entire seclusion from the life of this world cannot be presumed, in the case of any members of a Reformed and Protestant Church, which regards monasticism with a just suspicion, and fills its Book of Common Prayer with devotions and exhortations alike suited to and presupposing an intermixture in the daily life of this world. Can we say anything on this day's subject—Prayer in its relation to Action—which shall assist us who are here assembled in giving a practical character to our devotion, and a devout character to our life? God help us so to do!

We will say but two things.

1. Prayer is the Preparation for Action.

What Prayer is to Preaching, that is Action to Prayer; its end and goal. That Sermon is successful, which makes men pray: that Prayer is successful, which makes men act.

Now who has not often to lament that his Prayer does not lead to Action?

It is necessary indeed to remember that Action has a spiritual field as well as an outward. There is an action of the soul, which is the highest of all practical workings. That living energy of conscious and fervent love—love to God, and love to man—which goes forth in holy aspirations, charitable feelings and benevolent designs, is Action, and the noblest Action. There is a bodily, and there is also a spiritual exercise; of which the former profits little, and the latter much. Therefore when we speak of Prayer as a Preparation for Action, we do not speak only of that action which man sees, or of which man is the object. If Prayer rectifies the disorder of the spirit; if Prayer heals the soul's diseases; if Prayer makes me love God more earnestly, and hunger and thirst more keenly after righteousness, and take greater pleasure in God's Word and worship and Communion; if it makes me register in God's book of remembrance a vow of universal and individual forgiveness, and carry forth with me a soothed and softened feeling into the turmoil and irritation of my daily contact with mankind; then, in the same degree, it has had Action in view, and it has put forth its marvellous power upon just that department of action which is the spring of all; upon the condition of the feelings and affections, upon the temper of the spirit and the state of the soul.

But this is not all. And even with regard to this object of Prayer—the regulation of the in-

ward being, the calming and softening and sweet-
ening of the soul—how disappointing, oftentimes,
has been our experience! How shallow, how
transitory, how evanescent, has been that influence which we fondly hoped was deep and effectual! How has one vexing word made havoc of
the fancied tranquillity, and the dew of the morning devotion long before noon has passed by and
perished!

But although this kind of action is a legitimate
(and in one sense the highest) object of Prayer, it
is not the only one. Life is made up of single
particulars, both of doing and suffering, both of
sin and duty; and the Prayer which has respect
to it must be not vague and general, but particular
and even minute. The great enemy will assail
me to-day, not in some grand sweeping charge,
which every energy of my soul will be forewarned
and forearmed to encounter—but in detail; in a
multitude of light skirmishings and small am-
bushes, the very meaning of which will be often
doubtful, and their result apparently indecisive.
Yet is it in these things that the course of the life
shapes itself, and the destiny of the life is at
last determined. A succession of little defeatings

makes up at last a rout and a ruin. If I wait to
defend myself, till the imperial foe, in person and
presence, places himself at the head of his guards
and stakes all upon one last effort—the battle is
decided before it is waged, and the soul which
would not arm must pay the price in discomfiture.
So then, Prayer, which is the arming of the soul,
must have respect to the items of the conflict
even more than to the sum.   A vague petition for
grace—a general entreaty for God's strength and
protection through the day that is dawning—a
summary view of duty and temptation, and an
indiscriminating invocation of the enabling and
preserving Spirit—will not be found to have
brought God (so to speak) into the very heart and
body of the day's life : superficial prayer can look
only for a superficial answer; and the intentions
and resolutions of the slight asker are but *as tow
when it toucheth the fire,* in face of the wily strata-
gems or fiery onslaughts of *spiritual wickednesses in
high places.*   The Prayer which would affect
Action must be minute and detailed as well as
earnest.

God knows, indeed, what things we have need
of before we ask Him. Yet even for these will

He be enquired of. The man who cares not to bring to God the details of his wants and of his weaknesses, must either be indifferent or else presumptuous. Indifferent, if he grudges the time, the trouble, or the reflection, needful for spreading before the mercy-seat the programme of his perils. Presumptuous, if he would find God's help without seeking it; idly relying upon the promise, and utterly forgetful of the *asking* which must precede the *having*.

Long prayers, no doubt, may be lifeless: *much speaking*, Christ warns us, may be but the heathen man's *vain repetition:* yet He Himself who thus spake passed whole nights in Prayer, and His Apostle bids us all to *pray without ceasing.* Short prayers may avail much: God counts not, but weighs, man's supplications: and often has a miracle of grace been the response to a mere ejaculation of the godly. Yet this also is true— and the subject bids us ponder it—that prayer may be short and lifeless too; that infrequent prayer is a sign of indifference, and vague prayer a bar to the operations of grace. The more fully we spread out before God the day's action; its circumstances, known or suspected, of trial and difficulty; the special ways in which it is probable that temper will be provoked, and peace disturbed, and ambition roused, and vanity stimulated, and pride wounded; the particular snares which we foresee, in the form of murmuring, or indolence, or cowardice, or evil lusting; the stronger will be the proof of our heart's desire for the help of God, the surer the hope that the remembrance of Him will come with the temptation, and that He who *suffers us not to be tempted above that we are able*, will also on the instant *make a way* for us, and also incline us, *to escape*.

Nothing assuredly is so daunting to the soul's energies as the non-success of Prayer. To find ourselves, after what seemed to be honest asking, not receiving; after what seemed to be earnest knocking, not heard and not admitted; or to discover by the result that, after seeming to receive and seeming to be answered, we are yet as weak as ever in the moment of temptation—still turning our back when none pursueth, and giving way to the devil when a moment's resistance would have made him flee from us; this indeed is dreadful: what shall help if Prayer fails? If, after praying, we are as weak as if we prayed not—as slow to duty, as powerless against sin, as if all had been left to nature or inclination or casual impulse—what can become of us? Who shall help him whom God helps not—who has actually called upon God, and yet had no answer?

Therefore it is that we must so earnestly endeavour not to let Prayer fail us. Let us so pray as that we may obtain. Let not the thought enter, that God will not hear. The fault must be in the prayer, if it succeeds not. Search it out therefore, and spare not. Is it, perhaps, that prayer has been faint-hearted, wavering, faithless? Or is it, perhaps, that, though not insincere, it has been slight and vague and rare—entering into no particulars of our life—and too distant, one prayer from another, to connect God with all our doings? If this be so—and of whom is not this true in some measure?—then let us resolve, through grace, to remedy the fault while we may, by making our prayer more minute and more confiding; by placing ourselves more entirely in God's hands in it, making it our delight every day, and looking out (as it were) through the day for those successes and those victories in small things over self and sin, which shall assure us, by practical proof, that

God *has not cast out our prayer, nor turned His mercy from us.*

On the other hand, and in the last place, Action is the working-out of Prayer.

Some men make Action everything. They think that they can do for themselves all that is required of them on the part of God. They have never learned the lesson of weakness: they have never *seen the vision of God, nor known the knowledge of the Most High.* If they had stood where Moses stood on the mountain burning with fire ; if they had seen with Isaiah the glory of God in His temple, the seraphim chanting before Him the *Te Deum* of their ceaseless praise, and *the posts of the door moved at the voice of Him that cried;* they too would have exclaimed with him, *I am a man of unclean lips—for mine eyes have seen the King, the Lord of hosts.*

But this knowledge of themselves they have not, and therefore they are confident still and self-reliant. They still need the *live coal from off the altar,* the anointing fire of the Holy Spirit, that they may go forth in His strength from the communion of Prayer to the life of Action.

And others make Prayer everything. They so

misread the Divine promise, as to suffer it to make
them idle. When they have once prayed for grace,
they expect that grace to save them all trouble;
not only to work in them and to work with them,
but to work for them too. If any one speak to
them of the need of toil and the need of self-denial
and the need of vigilance, they more than half
suspect him of a self-righteous spirit, and think
that they have parried the exhortation, when they
have answered, *Christ is all.*

And Christ is all. Ill were it for us if He were
not. Those who know what they are, and what
their best effort is, and their most earnest exertion, and their most devout prayer, will certainly
echo the saying, *Christ is all, and in all.*

But even as the Prophet, when the live coal had
touched his lips, purging iniquity, heard the voice
of the Lord, saying, *Whom shall I send, and who
will go for us?* and answered, *Here am I, send me;*
so will the man of prayer, and the man to whom
Christ is all, go forth in the spirit of prayer and in
the strength of faith, to do the work of God, inward and outward, in his vocation: day by day,
he will carry forth with him, to the day's duties
and the day's temptations, the dew of grace and

the blessing of devotion : he will go forth as one whom God has sent, and whom God has commissioned, to do God's will and to set forth God's praise. The baptism of the Holy Ghost and of fire has been renewed to him this morning, and in the power of that grace he sets himself to the day's action, which is, in other words, the working-out of the day's Prayer. Expand the thought a little, and what is it?

First, he has received power. Prayer is a real thing to him, and the answer to Prayer is a real thing to him. He asked, asked in faith, asked earnestly—and God heard him. God has given him, he knows, the thing which he sought. God has *strengthened him with strength in his soul;* even with the living presence of the Holy Spirit, to be in him both a spring of comfort and a rock of strength.

Next, he has anticipated trial. It cannot take him by surprise. He has gone over, in God's presence, the probable conflicts, the foreseen diffi culties, of the hours which are to make up to-day. For these, as one by one they meet him, he is definitely equipped and harnessed : he has seen them before, in that holy place of the tabernacle where weakness is strength and timidity courage; and when they arrive, he can say, Here is that concerning which I prayed, and I know that that which I prayed against shall not hurt me. *Faithful is He that promised, who also will do it.* And if, as it may be, there are toils and struggles for me in the course of this day which I knew not of and named not; unexpected circumstances, or new complications, which vary the form at least, if not the nature, of my trial; yet over these also the prayer of faith shall have thrown unawares its protecting shield; the grace that is given me is not bare and scanty, but large and liberal in its measure: *Whensoever I call upon Thee, then shall mine enemies be put to flight: this I know; for God is on my side.*

Again, he acts in the spirit of Prayer. He has not ceased to pray when his morning prayer was ended. He looks upward still. He finds this quite necessary. The moment he trusts in past grace, or regards the answer to prayer as a thing given out of hand, his to reckon and to rely and to repose upon; and not rather as a living personal indwelling, which requires perpetual application and perpetual converse to make it avail-

ing for its purpose; that moment he finds himself all weakness, and *beginning to sink* must cry
out afresh, *Lord, save me.* The gift that is in
him must be stirred up perpetually: the cry of the
heart from amidst toil and temptation, must carry
on the prayer of faith, and apply the answer of
grace.

Lastly, he looks forward to the prayer of evening. It is a great help to him to remember that,
as he started from God's presence, so also he will
return to it. He has to go back at eventide with
his report and with his reckoning. Let him not
have to say then, Lord, I forgot Thee in earth's
interests: Lord, I failed to speak for Thee amidst
earth's companionships: Lord, I lightly regarded
Thee in comparison with this pleasure, that gain,
or this indulgence: Lord, when that old temptation came, I yielded, I fell: when that little exertion was needed, I let sloth conquer me: when
that soul opened itself to me for counsel or comfort, I took the honour, but I did not the work,
of Thy messenger. The Prophet goes back into
God's presence, and says, *Lord, who hath believed
my report?* The Apostles, returned from their
mission, *gather themselves together unto Jesus, to tell*

Him both what they have done and what they have taught. Even so must the humblest Christian close his commonest day, as he began it, with secret confession and renewed supplication. I say that from the midst of his day's labour and warfare he looks forward to that still hour of evening prayer, and prepares for it by exertion and by faithfulness through the daytime. The prospect of prayer is powerful with him like its retrospect. He would fain be able to close the day, not in depression but in thankfulness; not as a vanquished man, but as one who *has done all and stands;* as one whom his Lord, when He comes back from the far journey or from the midnight wedding, shall find still watching—his loins girded about and his lamp burning.

Alas! the report of no earthly day can be for any man all joyous. Duties ill done, half done, or left undone; sins of temper and spirit, of thought and word, yea, of act also; shortcomings, unfaithfulnesses, murmurings, backslidings; these things crowd the evening's devotion, even as the prayer against them was the staple of the morning's. Shall it be always thus? Shall life itself, at its close, be to us what its separate days are?

Shall we have to say against ourselves then, as now, Unprofitable, unfaithful, inconsistent, unclean?

Let us anticipate that last evening; that lying down, not for sleep, but in death. Let us arouse ourselves, by grace, to this duty, this mercy, this blessing, of Prayer. If God says to us, as He says now, *Seek ye my face;* let us be ready with the answer, every one of us, *Thy face, Lord, will I seek.* The man of Prayer is he who lives well: the man of Prayer is he who will die happy.

V

PRAYER A DISCIPLINE AND AN EDUCATION.

"Thy loving correction shall make me great."—Ps. xviii. 35.

THE two words Discipline and Education might be made synonymous. Education is Discipline. Discipline is Education. And thus our subject might be charged with tautology, and shortened with advantage into Prayer a Discipline, or Prayer an Education, instead of introducing both terms, Prayer a Discipline and an Education.

And if we give to Discipline its more usual sense, then it might be called a part of Education; and thus a different kind of inaccuracy might be discovered in the title, a Discipline and an Education.

But I trust that the subject proposed to us, if

not quite exact in its terms, may yet serve its purpose; which is, to show how Prayer is an appointed instrument for man's good, as a being designed for a higher and nobler condition, needing a preparatory process of training for its eventual realization.

And in speaking upon this great topic, so large and grand that it needs limiting and coercing on all sides to make it possible to deal with it in any way, I have chosen two words, out of many, to guide our thoughts; understanding now by Discipline that process which is carried on in a School, and by Education that process which is carried on in a Home; the one the training of a Master's authority, the other the rearing of a Parent's love. The Schoolmaster disciplines: the Parent educates. Let us, in that order, though perhaps an inverted order—for the home comes in point of time before the school—reflect upon the twofold training which God offers to carry on in each one of us by means of His marvellous and most merciful ordinance of Prayer.

1. Prayer a Discipline.

We have heard of Schools in which the instruction was good, but the discipline bad. It is in that sense that I use the word now. What do we mean by good and bad discipline in a school? We mean nothing imaginary, nothing fanciful, nothing (to a practised observer) ambiguous. An experienced visitor feels rather than argues the presence or the absence of this characteristic. As he enters, as he glances round, as he stands there neither interfering nor seeming to notice, he is cognizant, he is conscious, of the net result of the master's attention or inattention, of the master's skill or want of skill, through a year past, in refer- ence to one branch, to one half (and not the smaller half) of his duty. There is in the one case a readiness, a promptitude, an alacrity of response to the first signal of command or of prohibition; a thoroughness, a completeness, a per- fection, of obedience ; a kind of electric or magi- cal intercommunion between the mind that wills and the minds that obey, which at once secures the performance, and yet takes out of it the whole idea of constraint or terror. That is a faint sketch of a school in good discipline.

And need I describe the opposite? A general sense of unpunctuality, tardiness, slovenliness, in- completeness ; a constant wear and tear, on both sides, of much speaking and little doing; an air, on the one hand, of vain ordering, empty threatening, or helpless beseeching; an air, on the other hand, of simple indifference, good-humoured defiance, or furtive ridicule.

No one, looking on this picture and on that, will doubt afterwards the connection between instruction and discipline, or maintain again the foolish fallacy that persuasion can entirely take the place of rule.

Such is discipline in human hands; so necessary, so potent, so beneficent in its saving of trouble and in its clearing of the way for knowledge.

Now we have all heard of the discipline of life. It is a common figure which describes this world as a vast school, in which men are placed, for the whole of their threescore years and ten, or fourscore years, to learn wisdom by experience, and (may we not add in inspired language?) *obedience by suffering*.

The essence of Discipline is the schooling of the will: the correction of the natural pride, so that it shall recognize another existence and obey a higher law; the existence and the law of Him

in whom all *live and move and have their being.*
Discipline is the subjugation of the self-will to the
will of One higher and greater and more excellent
than it. And this subjugation, of which a well-
ordered school furnishes an earthly type, is the
object—as believing men feel—of all that system
and course of the individual life which is as uni-
form in its principle as it is multifarious in its
working.

No two lives are alike in their details. Seldom
can you even declare two lives exactly equal in the
sum total of their joys and sorrows. And yet we
believe that, when the great principle of the Divine
compensation is put to them, most lives—it may
be, all lives—will have been equitably measured
out for trial and for blessing. But let that question pass. *Shall not the Judge of all the earth do
right ?* This we say—that every life has had in
it a scheme and an object : that scheme, the
arrangement of circumstances by a special as well
as omnipotent Providence ; that object, the bringing of the self-will first into captivity, and then at
last into conformity, to the all-wise, all-holy, and
all-loving will of God. That object is the key,
faith being the judge, to all the thwartings and

crossings, all the humiliations and mortifications, all the bruisings and crushings, of desire and inclination, in the present state of being: for all these, from the further side, the redeemed and ransomed will give equal and perpetual praise, when the Lord *binds up the breach of His people, and heals the stroke of their wound.*

But our present remark is, that, just what life is, in this respect, as a whole, that the particular ordinance of Prayer is as a part: not Life only, but Prayer, is a Discipline.

Here our appeal lies to experience.   We speak to those who pray—to those who know something of Prayer beyond its lifeless form—and to these we would say, first,

Is not Prayer a constant humiliation of the self-will?

Of course it is meant to be so.   In prayer, our spirit ought to be always, what our language will often be, *Thy will, O God, not mine, be done.*

But this is not all, nor the chief part of the self-mortification of Prayer.   This is a voluntary humbling : we speak now rather of the involuntary; of that which more directly thwarts and brings us low in our own eyes.

Prayer is a discipline, because it shows us what we are; how infirm of purpose, how irresolute in self-control, how impotent even to feel as we would, even to desire that which we know we want.

Is it indeed true but of one or two amongst us, or is it not rather the experience, more or less, of all, that prayer is a constant difficulty, a perpetual struggle, not only in the sense in which St Paul speaks of striving, wrestling, combating in prayer for his congregations, but rather in this way, that we have to do battle first with ourselves, in order to pray at all? That we kneel down reluctant, tongue-tied, indifferent; drag forth petitions *as with a cart-rope;* feel not the evils which we want to deplore, or desire not those good things which alone God offers? Do not some hearts echo the experience, and confess that, if there be such a thing anywhere as an instrument of self-humiliation, Prayer is that discipline—that never do we see so much of the earthliness, wilfulness, and depravity of our own nature, as when we most of all expect to be free from it—when we are professing to seek God's presence, and to practise ourselves for the life beyond? A man who would know what he is, must bring himself to the touchstone of Prayer.

There is this also. Discipline—whether it be God's discipline or man's, the discipline of a school or the discipline of a life—is carried on principally by a system of punishments and rewards. It is an affectation to dispense with them. God Himself largely uses them, in training the childhood (and in this life we are all children) of His redeemed. They are a part of the scaffolding of the moral being; not to be taken down till we shall have reached hereafter, through grace, *the measure of the stature of the fulness of Christ.*

Now Prayer is a discipline of punishment and of reward.

In many senses: but in this one certainly. Every transgression is punished, every victory is rewarded, through the instrumentality of Prayer. As long as conscience has life in it—and when conscience is quite dead, there will be no praying —it is a sore judgment to return to prayer after sinning. To go back to God with this blot, old perhaps yet new, upon me; to return to Him at evening to say, That sin against which I prayed this morning, I have sinned yet again—that effort for which I asked strength this morning, I refused and rejected when the time came—that evil thought, that censorious word, that selfish, sensual, cruel act, which Thou forgavest me yesterday when I desired Thee, I have thought it, I have said it, I have done it, yet again, turning my profession of sorrow into hypocrisy, my very prayer into a sin—to have this to do, and not once nor twice, but perpetually, till we could almost cease to pray, for very mortification and shame—is it not a severe chastisement, a heavy punishment, for our sins? What are sackcloth and ashes to it? Is not that Prayer, which thus punishes, in the most obvious sense a Discipline?

And to be able—does it ever happen to us?—to give in to God at evening a better report; to be able to say, Amidst many shortcomings, inconsistencies, and falls this day, I have found Thy grace sufficient for me in the matter of that thing of which I spake to Thee—Thy strength, perfected in my weakness, checked the rude retort, calmed the hot anger, quenched the fiery dart of lust, and left me, when the battle ended at nightfall, still standing—to Thee, O God, not to me, be all the praise—this surely is a discipline of reward, as the other was of punishment : this shall help the good fight to-morrow : this shall prove to me that there is such a thing as grace Divine, a Saviour ready to succour, and a God that heareth Prayer!

And this discipline of Prayer is itself what the text calls a *loving* correction.   Not only is it a preparation for that other life which shall be all love : it is already, in proportion to its efficacy, comfort and peace.   In this third point also it is rightly named a Discipline.

We spoke of good discipline in a school as saving trouble.   Discipline, true discipline, is essentially beneficent. Anarchy is always misery. While it is an open question, which is the stronger, the nominal subject or the lawful ruler, so long there is no peace : it is excluded.   When once a firm hand has secured allegiance ; when the rebellion of the self-will is prevented by a foreknowledge of its own weakness ; how much more, when the will of the superior has become the will of the inferior, and long experience of wisdom and goodness has wrought on the other side an unquestioning trust which only yearns to obey ; then the fruit of discipline is seen in *quietness and assurance for ever :* warfare is ended, rest is begun : wisdom can utter her voice, and the ear of ignorance is opened to listen.

Even thus is it with the holy discipline of Prayer. *Thy loving correction shall make me great.* Sin felt to be misery—holiness found to be happiness— what shall hinder the progress of that soul in communion with Him whom to know is life, whom to serve is perfect freedom?

2. Prayer an Education.

It was an old error, now exploded, to confound Education with Instruction. It matters little, indeed, what word is used—and words are often transferred by custom from one sense to another— if the thing intended be clear. But the mischief of this misuse was, that a parent sending his child to a school for a few hours perhaps of the day, fancied himself to have provided for his whole training; washed his hands altogether of an intransferable responsibility, and thought it a hard thing and a culpable thing if the schoolmaster did not return him to him perfect, every bad influence, even of his home, counteracted, and the boy effectually warranted for a life of success and virtue.

Education is not instruction. The best-instructed man in the world might be the worst-

P

educated. Education is the bringing up. Education is the training for life. Education is the calling out of powers, the strengthening of faculties, the counteraction of faults, the controlling and coercing of vices, the preparation of the whole man for the whole of being, the presentation of body, soul, and spirit, equipped for the work of time and for the enjoyment of eternity.

This is a work which the parent cannot depute. This rearing and bringing up—this preparation of the whole man for the whole of being—is far more the work of home than the work of school: perhaps, if we knew all, we should find that the years of childhood have in them the germ of the eternal being, and that in most cases, in a sense far beyond that in which the famous words were uttered, *the child is*, in deed and in truth, *father of the man.*

Education, in its simplest practical definition, is the formation of a life's habits under direction. It is in this sense that we use the words now, and say that Prayer is an Education.

Habits are of two chief kinds. There are habits of thought, and there are habits of action.

It is through habit that knowledge is implanted. The knowledge of a language is the result of long association of signs and things signified. The word is the token of a thing : repeated use, under direction, connects in my mind the symbol and the interpretation : at last I can infer with rapidity the one from the other, or substitute each for each, almost with the facility of one who spoke that tongue from his birth.

It is through habit that principles are formed. A high and holy motive is first suggested as a novelty to the child. He is told that it ought to be his, or he sees it to be another's : it is lodged within him as a possibility : he tries it as an experiment : he acquiesces in it as a satisfaction : at last it comes to him as a use. Or a bad and wicked idea is communicated. At first it comes to him as a surprise, perhaps shocks him as a horror : but it lodges itself, it familiarizes itself : he sees others admit, accept, practise it, and nothing follows : it ceases to repel, it begins to attract : at last he too follows the influence, and does evil. These things are the experiences of all observers and of all actors. It was thus that conduct was gradually shaped, it was thus that character eventually formed itself, in you, and in me, and in all men.

And this then was Education. It was the formation of a life's habits.

And that, under direction. We cannot say how it might be with a solitary man—without associates and without instructors. For ourselves, and speaking generally, we can trace up our good and our evil to some influence. Even the poor neglected orphan, whose school has been the street, has formed his habits too under direction; the direction not of the wise and good, but of the waifs and strays of society, the more persuasive in their influences because the things to which they invited *were only evil continually*.

All God's dealings with us are of the nature of an Education.

God educated the world by a succession of Divine Revelations, training it gradually, by elements and rudiments, by types and symbols, by precepts and prophecies, for the full illumination of the Gospel and of the Spirit. He formed habits in man, of thought and judgment, of principle and action, that He might bring him out at last, in the fulness of grace and knowledge, to be His representative and His witness on an earth too long debased by his Fall and defiled by his sin.

And God educates each man by a system of personal dealing, of which the characteristic is the same : it is an Education : it is a formation of habits, whether of thought or action, under the direction of His Providence, His Word, His Church, His Spirit.

And Prayer is one chief part of this Education.

(1) Look at it in reference to the final end of being.

By a certain day, not far distant for the youngest, each one of us must be ready for a stupendous change. We must be prepared for that mysterious, that awful transition—from a world seen to a world unseen—from a life of which the interests are experience, to a life of which our every conception is an act of faith.

What the life of mature age in this world is to the child learning his Alphabet or the boy struggling with his grammar, that is the life after death to the eldest and the wisest man below : something for which he is being prepared, almost in the dark, by a process the meaning of which he knows not, or knows only by an effort of filial reliance upon the wisdom and love of One to whom he owes his being.

Now if he is to be ready, without further interval or training, to enter at death upon the occupations of a world invisible and immaterial—a world in which there shall be neither indulgence of appetite, nor hoarding of money, nor ambition of fame, nor vanity nor luxury nor creature-worship, but only the spirits of just men made perfect, and an innumerable company of Angels, and God the Judge of all, and Jesus the Mediator of a new Covenant; so that he who loves not these things, even if he could be admitted, would not care to enter—must there not be an Education for that world? Must there not be a formation of those habits which will be all in all then? some anticipation, by spiritual intercourse now, of a life so strange to flesh and blood—insomuch that we may people that world with loving friends and congenial companionships, and be able at once, when we reach it, to enjoy its pleasures and to set our hand to its employments?

That Education, that anticipation, is Prayer. In Prayer, earnest Prayer, we exist, for the time, even now, in the things of eternity and of heaven. We form the habit, and practise the habit, of realizing and communicating with a world not seen.

We learn to disconnect the two ideas, real, and visible. We should not kneel thus, nor thus speak, nor thus confess and praise and pray, if there were not some One out of sight who is all-wise and all-mighty and all-good; if there were not interests more engrossing, and works more important, and pleasures more satisfying, than those of earth and time; if there were not counsels formed, and plans laid, and powers operating, quite apart from and above the relations of human society and the arrangements of confederate kings; nor if we ourselves had no part nor lot in those everlasting realities of which the shadows only and the phantoms are here.

(2) Prayer is the Education of thought and action for the final end of being. But there is yet one thing more. A man educated for *that world* must be educated also for this. The realities of the eternal future must be anticipated now: *the powers of the world to come* must be *tasted,* an Apostle writes, and *partaken of,* here. Human impatience is sometimes eager to go : but the call of God, meanwhile, is to glorify Him, as did Christ, on the earth.

There is not, in the records of Inspiration, that

sharp line of distinction, which man loves to widen
and deepen, between the Christian life below and
the Divine life above. Crucified with Christ
already, buried with Christ, and risen with
Christ already—already in heaven where Christ
is, the affections set above, and the true life hid-
den there with Christ in God—living because
Christ lives, and having both the Father and the
Son to abide with him through the Spirit—such is
the language of Holy Scripture in reference to the
condition of the Christian man in the time that is.
It is an ideal—it is a principle—it is an ambition
even more than an attainment—a progressive not
a sudden work of renewal and sanctification. For
it too, as well as for the life of glory, there is an
Education—and the chief instrument of that Education is Prayer. He who would know what the
life of Christ is must pray and not faint. He must
bring God into his life below, by carrying up his
life every day to God above. In proportion as he
acquires the habit of communication and communion with Christ in heaven—not in the brief
perfunctory prayer of him who cares not if he be
never answered—not in the summary asking of a
few particular blessings, which a man might even

have and be little profited—but rather in the
earnest desire to live with Christ and to have
Christ for his life ; in the same degree will his
Education for both worlds advance apace : men
here will see his light shine, and glorify God :
and death, when it comes, will be but the unveil-
ing of a presence long lived in, the actual admission into the sight of Him whom not having seen
He has yet through long years both known and
loved.

And what shall I more say ?

The praises of Prayer are one thing : the experiences of Prayer are another.

No man in this thing can deliver his brother,
nor make agreement unto God for him. Prayer
is the cry of the individual soul, to a God personally needed.

O, while the evil days come not—days of bitter
sorrow, days of overwhelming temptation—days
of resistless passion, sudden fall, and life-long ruin
—remember thy Creator, and have Him for thy
Friend! Young men, strong in all else—strong
in health and spirits, strong in the confidence of
character and in the imagination of your own
stedfastness—be strong, I beseech you, yet in

this one thing besides—a life guarded by God, and a soul consigned to His keeping! Weak at the best, is the house built on the sand—the sand of nature, of disposition, of resolution, of self: when the rain descends, when the flood comes, when the winds blow and beat upon it, great, great is its fall! And strong, strong above telling, is the house built upon the rock—the rock of faith, the rock of prayer—the rock of Christ, which is the rock of God! Upon that house may throw itself, with all its influence or with all its fury, the wave of ill persuasion, the flood of evil example, the blast of unkindness, the tempest of temptation—it falls not, for God is there!

Happy are the people that are in such a case ; yea, blessed are the people who have the Lord for their God !

HUMAN LIFE.

I

THE SON FRETTING AGAINST THE RESTRAINTS OF HIS HOME.

"Yea, hath God said, Ye shall not eat of every tree of the garden?"—GEN. iii. 1.

THE *son of Adam, which was the son of God,* is the climax, in St Luke's Gospel, of the human genealogy of Jesus. Adam was in right of creation—a right as yet clear and unforfeited—a son of God. And this son, like other sons, had a home; a home in the blessed Paradise, watered by its four streams, and enlightened by a supernatural Presence. And that home, like other homes, had its restraints as well as its blessings. There stood just one tree in the very midst of the garden, concerning which it was said to him, *Thou shalt not eat of it. In the*

day that thou eatest thereof thou shalt surely die.
And the text tells how there arose—we know not
whether late or early, for the flight of years is un-
marked in the paradisiacal blessedness—a fretting
of this son against the restraints, against this one
restraint, of his home ; how the fallen spirit used
this as the engine of his first assault upon man's
innocence, making him ponder the fact and question the reasonableness of this single prohibition
by which the Almighty Father asserted His sovereignty over the child whom He had formed and
the earth which He had created.

Thus the third chapter of the Bible furnishes
the appropriate text for our present meditation, of
which the thesis is—

*The son fretting against the Restraints of his
Home.*

His Home.   The word Home is full of restful
thoughts and tender associations.   The family, of
which home is the centre, is God's primary and
original ordinance.   There was a family before
there was a state : there was a family before there
was a Church.   Out of family life grew naturally
all other modes of being—social, civil, political,
ecclesiastical.   For long ages the family was the

Church; and the birthright of the firstborn in-
cluded the priesthood and the intercession. If
the stream of civilization should ever flow back
upon itself—if factitious inequalities should be
levelled, political institutions overthrown, the
Church itself (so far as it rests upon outward supports) demolished and done away—there would
still be the source and spring of all, so long as
there is the Home: there might man still love,
and there might the universal Father still be worshipped.

Even as it is, while the complications of society
continue as we have them, the deepest of all
truths, the most real of all facts, the most stable
and solid of all relations, is that of the family, that
of the home. It begins earlier, it strikes deeper,
it penetrates more thoroughly the whole fabric of
the being, than any other influence or any other
reality. If a home is corrupt, woe to the life! If
a father's character, if a mother's example, cannot
be depended upon, where is the new cruse, where
is the healing salt, which shall give back its sparkling vitality to that spring of the waters? Even
without this worst supposition, who has not noticed
the injurious effect upon a young life, upon the

character of a man throughout life, to have had, from circumstances, no home—to have been deprived, by death, or by a separation like death, of the enjoyment, of the use, of the possession, of a home?

Children, young men, grown men, value your homes! Give God daily thanks for them. Little do you know—for these are blessings seldom appreciated till they are withdrawn—all that is contained for you—all of safety, all of happiness, all of blessing—within the four walls of your home.

But now this Home, of which such glorious things are spoken, and of which we have not told one thousandth part of its mercies—this home is a society, this home is a polity, is a little state, is a little Church. Then, like other societies, it must have its rules; like other polities, it must have its laws. And rules are restraints. They are, so far as they go, limitations upon the self-will. They are conditions upon which alone the benefits of the community can be enjoyed. Where is the home which has no laws? which imposes no restrictions upon its members—whether natural members, the children—or acquired and temporary, like its hired servants? That home cannot be safe ; that home cannot be happy. There must be restraints upon the free will of each, if there is to be any security, or if there is to be any comfort, for the body, which is the whole. In these days it is the fashion to relax rules. Homes try to dispense with restraints. Each child, from the first beginning of speech, is to express his own opinion : each child, from the first power of motion, is to do his own will. Entreaty replaces command, and persuasion supersedes authority. Does happiness result from this sort of freedom ? If there was once too much of distance between the parents and the children, may there not easily be too little ? Is it to be desired that the father and his son should (as it is sometimes avowed, sometimes even boasted) live together like brothers ? This is an inversion of God's order ; and God's order can never be changed without mischief and without suffering. In place of authority, plainly asserted and gravely maintained, there will always grow up something else ; something more unequal, more uncertain, more trying and irritating therefore to all ; hasty snatchings of the reins from time to time, as temper, or caprice, or experience of inconvenience, may dictate : and thus the self-

Q

will, which might have been gradually disciplined into obedience, kicks against the sudden goad of an occasional interference ; and the son, who would have borne the light burden and easy yoke of an equable subordination, frets against the unexpected thwartings of a restraint at once violent and unprincipled.

But our present subject should remind us rather of a fretting against home restraints, which has no such excuse to palliate it. It does happen—such is fallen nature—even to a wise and loving father, to have, in the best of homes, an unamiable and a disobedient son. There is a vast difference—who can gainsay it?—between the natural dispositions, tempers, and temptations of different persons. In one point of view, this is a great mystery. Where is the equality of God's government, even in moral and spiritual things? Where is that reconciling harmonizing principle which shall make compensation for what we cannot but call the diverse advantages of one and another, even for obedience, even for morality, even for salvation? We must leave these questions in the hands of God. *Shall not the Judge of all the earth do right ? Shall the thing formed say to Him that formed it, Why hast*

Thou made me thus ? This we know already—
that no one need be wicked. The struggle may
seem to be more severe for one than for another;
but God *giveth more grace* as man needs more, and
will most surely give enough of His grace to every
one who asks Him.

Meanwhile every home has its restraints, and
the undutiful son frets against them.

He is impatient of its indirect, unexpressed,
understood restrictions. He feels himself ill at
ease in that presence in which an irreverent expression would be an insult, and an impure jest an
impossibility; in which, whatever he may be elsewhere, he cannot possibly introduce any thing or
any person but that which is decent and honourable
and of good report.

And he is impatient also of its more direct
rules. What is the use, he asks, of this punctu-
ality of hours, this enforcement of particular times
for meals and prayers, for resting and rising; this
displeasure at an occasional lateness; this rigid
compulsion of my presence within doors before
a certain striking of the clock at evening? Am
I not old enough—and the question is asked early
—to have a little control over my own going and

coming, over my presence here or there, over my companionships and choice of friends? Another, whom I know, is not thus watched and guarded : why should I particularly be thus under suspicion and inspection? Surely it is time that I should be more trusted : nay—for such is the addition sometimes made to the argument of the self-deceiver—it would be better even for the development of my character that I should be more let alone.

And so it comes to pass, year after year, in the million homes of England, that the story of the sacred Parable is again and again acted : the son says to his father, in thought if not in words, Give me my portion and let me begone ! the days of childhood are past ; the time of self-reliance, the time of self-responsibility, the time of liberty and independence, is come ! Oh, we often hear it : and always—whether it be said in words, or only shown in the manner, in the look, in the tell-tale countenance—whenever we perceive it, we tremble !

It is the fashion of the times to indulge this spirit. From an early age, in many towns, the son only lodges with his parents ; pays his rent, pays for his board, like any stranger ; and if a word of reproof or remonstrance is uttered, will even change his lodging and be gone! The son frets against the restraints of his home, and if these restraints be reduced to a mere shadow, he will rebel against them and he will resent them still.

But was it then for the sake of a discourse on family life—its blessings, its trials, and its sorrows —that we chose the subject now before us? *These things are an allegory.* What we see in human homes is a type of what God sees in the great human home every day. And thus we find ourselves in the very heart of a deeply spiritual subject, through which may God guide us to some serious reflections, and to an earnest amendment of life.

The Son spoken of is, like Adam, a son of God.

I know that there are persons who would deny this. The creation claim of sonship, they say, is lost and gone : it is only by individual conversion that any one now can be a son of God. I do not quite think so. I think that in a true sense every created being, who has reason, and who has a soul, is a son of God. I think that in a yet higher sense every redeemed person—and is not redemption co-extensive with mankind?—is a son of God.

And I think that, in a sense closer and more personal still, every one who is made a member of the Christian Church by Baptism, is a son and child of God. *We are compelled by the Christian verity* so to speak. Sonship in this application is, of course, in some degree a figure: but we have the warrant of Scripture for this threefold use of it; and it has a meaning, and it has a reality, and it has a power in it, in every one and in all of these applications. *When ye pray, say, Our Father*—without stopping to ask whether you, personally and individually, have entirely lived and felt and acted towards Him as a son. No man by well-doing can earn for himself a father: nor can any man, by any undutifulness, quite cease to be a son. Even the prodigal, even in the far country, could say still, *I will arise and go to my father.* Undutiful, disobedient, exile, outcast, he was a son still.

So then I say, concerning each one of us, that there is a true claim and a real relation of sonship involved in these three things combined—Creation, Redemption, Baptism. We are all God's children: we have all a place in God's home.

What is the Home? We might call the earth a home of God: so minute is His providence over

it, so wonderful its marks of His presence, so near
to every one of us the very Person of Him in
whom we all live and move and have our being.
We might call each family a home of God: so
marvellous, so life-like, is the representation and
reproduction, in each, of some features of the
Divine likeness; so instructive the working, in
these poor, faint, feeble imitations, of His over-
sight, His governance, His love. But far more
correctly do we designate the Church as God's
Home and Household; using the very language
of Scripture, and speaking now of a presence not
natural, but spiritual; not of mere superintendence
and governance, but of influence and inhabitation
—of inworking both to will and to do—of indwelling both to cheer and to quicken, both to
sanctify and to enable and to transform. *Whose
house,* the Scripture says, *are we. I will dwell in
them, and walk in them. I will be a Father unto
you, and ye shall be my sons and daughters, saith
the Lord Almighty.*

Thus then we have the son, and we have the
home. We have the House of God, which is the
Church of the living God: a society, not nominal
but real: a vast body of living people, receiving

the Bible as their book of truth, acknowledging
Christ as their only Saviour and only Lord, signed
and sealed as His in holy Baptism, assembling
themselves together to worship on the strength of
His work and promise, and celebrating from time
to time, in the congregation, that second special
ordinance of His institution, which is the sacrament of the Life, as the other was the sacrament
of the Regeneration. These are the sons, and
this is the home, spoken of in our subject. And
we are all of us—not by profession only, but by
right and title—inside that home, children of that
family. God has made us so, by promise and
providence, by word and ordinance, by the call of
His Gospel and by the sacrament of His conse-
cration. I beseech you not to deal with Him so
unthankfully as to doubt this. Do not choose the
outer darkness. Do not deny or gainsay that
Divine relationship which, without merit or quest
of yours, God Himself has bestowed upon you.
Do not say, God is not my Father, because I do
not feel towards Him as a son should : God has
not brought me into His home, because I find
myself fretting against its rules and against its restrictions. This is not humility : this is rather the

mask of pride, and the expression of a churlish unfilial independence.

The work of humility is not this. Humility is not shown in saying, God has not done for me this or this; God has not taken me for His son, nor set upon me the seal of the inheritance and the adoption. Rather is humility seen in this other and most opposite confession—God has done all this for me, and I would not! God took me for His own child by adoption, and I fretted against Him and would none of Him! Yes, there is room enough for humility there! And this is a wholesome and genuine humility, as the other is morbid, and spurious, and untrue.

The home of God then, in the third place, has its restraints. Every one who would dwell within God's family is bound to keep its rules. Like other homes, it has its hours of refreshment and worship, its conditions of conduct and companionship, its regulations of speech and work, its requirements of duty, and its punishments of transgression. And all these things, though good in themselves, are of the nature of checks and thwartings to the fallen Adam.

Take an example or two.

The life of the soul depends upon communion with God. The Gospel invites us to the free and loving exercise of this communion. The ordinance of prayer, in private and in the congregation —the ordinance of devout study of God's Word —the ordinance of self-examination and meditation in holy things—the ordinance of humble and regular participation in the sacrament of the Lord's Supper—all these are delights and privileges to the established Christian : but they are commands and duties too ; rules of the Divine household, restraints upon that unbounded exercise of the free will which cannot be trusted to know its own good, or to seek its own good, without direction and without compulsion from the Head and Lord of the Church. All these things begin as duties for most men : by degrees they become habits, and then by degrees they become pleasures. But for most men they begin by being acts of obedience, rendered in reliance upon promise and in gratitude for redemption.

Now who is there who has not fretted sometimes against these rules of the Home ? Where is the young man who has not often departed—departed sometimes for long seasons—from the rule of prayer? Where is he who has not said in his heart, This necessity of devotion is irksome—let it alone? Sons of the house—if indeed Redemption and Baptism make us so—are absent for years and months from the meals, from the refreshments, of the family: the Lord's Table is almost empty of its guests, and the daily prayers of the Home are deserted utterly by the children.

It needs a second adoption—it needs a conversion, most often, even for those who never were aliens—to recall the unruly, the disobedient son, from a wandering which has been all inside the Home.

Again, our Lord Jesus Christ has distinctly warned us of the need of abstinence, on the part of God's children, from all those fleshly and sinful lusts which (an Apostle says) *war against the soul.* This is one of the rules, one of the restraints, of the Home. Yet who is there who submits himself readily, thoroughly, and of a glad will, to this severe self-discipline? How many are they who say in their hearts, Why this extreme strictness? why may not I, like other men, just taste at least, just enjoy for a season, the pleasures of sin? why strain to this uttermost limit the conditions of

Christianity and the Gospel? A short time shall suffice me: but for a short time, or, if not in act, yet in thought, let me know what it is to be my own master, to be trusted, to be free! Yes, it is the old story: the tempter comes to us still, as he came in Eden, with the insidious suggestion, *Yea, hath God said, Ye shall not eat of every tree of the garden?* Is it so, that the Creator, that the Redeemer, has hemmed you in with these restrictions of speech and action, when He knows all the while that, if you were but free from those fetters, you might be as gods, knowing good and evil? Ah! if He wished your happiness—if He desired the development of your whole being in the limitless regions of power and gladness, He would have left no one tree under the ban of this arbitrary prohibition: He would have allowed you, He would have bidden you to eat, without stint or precaution, of the tree of knowledge and of the tree of life!

The son listens, O how readily! and frets thenceforth against the restraints of his home.

One other reflection springs out of the former.

A watchful home is obliged to use some caution as to the admission of books. It is one part of the duty—not always attended to—of a Christian parent, to watch over the literature which is in large part to form the principles, as well as to gratify the taste, of the young. There lies a serious responsibility upon the heads of each family, to maintain a sufficient familiarity with the current writings of the day, to be able to say with decision and with intelligence, This book shall not enter my doors, and this other shall be welcome. In general, there is both an ignorant exclusion, and then, on the other side, as its natural accompaniment, a no less ignorant admission. It must be so. All parents are not readers : and all readers are not judges.

But the experience itself illustrates one of the restraints of the Divine Home. The narrative of man's life in Paradise seems to indicate to us a restriction even then upon his knowledge. The one tree from which he was debarred was the tree of knowledge of good and evil. Of that tree man has eaten ; and by reason of it *sin entered into the world, and death by sin.* But yet, though it be too late to keep from any man the general knowledge of evil, it is not too late to limit and fence for each man the familiarity with what Holy

Scripture calls *the depths of Satan.* Such knowledge is not necessary for us : conscience will
warn us, without minute foresight, when danger is
threatening : the knowledge of the mystery of evil
is not needful, and it is in itself debasing and de-
filing.   Let the son of God's House keep not only
the conscience, but (so far as it may be) the understanding pure.   If fallen nature frets under the
restraint, let the ambition of grace answer it.   If
I through mercy am to be (as God promises) a
partaker of the Divine nature, I must flee away, in
its every form, from the corruption that is in the
world through lust !

It is of the first risings of discontent within
against the restraints of God's Home that we speak
now.   We are not to tell now of the flight nor of
the exile.   We are only to seek to awaken, through
grace, the wholesome dread of murmuring, even
in thought, against the safeguards with which God
has surrounded us.   Let us say to ourselves, when
prayer is irksome to us, when the Bible refuses to
open—when some sinful thought seems pleasant,
when the companionship of an unprincipled friend
looks at once joyous and harmless—when some
difficult duty has to be done, or some strong in-

clination to be striven with unto the death—let us say to ourselves then, This is the mark of my being in God's Home : I have to do this, I have to bear this, against my natural wish, just because I have the joy and the glory of being one of Christ's redeemed, one of God's sons : this little struggle, this severe conflict, is a sign that I am on the way to glory. I will not fret against the restraints of my home, but rather bless God for everything which He makes a sign and proof of my sonship ; praying Him not to suffer me to depart from His house, but to dwell there all my brief lifetime, setting forth His praise, and receiving more and more upon my soul the likeness and the impress of His glory! *One thing have I desired of the Lord; that will I seek after: that I may dwell in the house of the Lord all the days of my life, to behold the beauty of the Lord, and to enquire in His temple.* So, *when my father and my mother forsake me, the Lord will take me up.* So, *when the earthly house of this tabernacle is dissolved*, I shall *have a building of God—an house not made with hands, eternal in the heavens.*

II

THE FUGITIVE SEEKING FREEDOM IN A FAR COUNTRY.

" But Jonah rose up to flee unto Tarshish from the presence
of the Lord."—JONAH i. 3.

HUS *the Son fretting against the Restraints of his Home* becomes, in the second place, *the Fugitive seeking Freedom in a far Country.* How often, during the six millenniums of earth's history, has this experience been verified, over and over again, in human hearts and in human homes ! The son has said to his father, Give me my portion ; and then has taken his journey to enjoy that inheritance in freedom. Or the son has not even said this, or said anything ; but has just made his escape from employments which were monotonous, and from influences which were irksome. Many a home has been desolated—many a parent's age has been brought down with sorrow to the grave—by reason of such undutifulness and such wilfulness. Some slight interference, some reasonable (or, be it so, some hasty) rebuke, overnight, has been followed—alas for the selfishness of the young!—by a stealthy night departure, and by long years of untracked wandering and of cruel heartless silence. The young man has enlisted himself as a soldier—or he has found a ship going to this colony or that foreign shore : he has *paid the fare thereof* and gone aboard. It is an old story. Now and then, but very seldom, success and fame have crowned it : a man once a fugitive from his father's home, has risen into eminence and opulence through his exile, and has lived to write himself a page in history ; the history of his country, or the history of his Church. Far more often the undutifulness of youth has fulfilled itself in the misery of manhood : evil habits, formed early, have borne fruit, long and late, in wretchedness and ruin : or, if not long and late, this has been because the great sinner is commonly a short-lived man ; because, if a man will not turn, judgment must bend its bow, and a God long mocked must at last interpose for punishment.

Thus viewed, the subject is a sad one : it must be so. But this is not precisely the treatment

designed for it to-day. Circumstances have forbidden any formal or elaborate dissection of the
terms or combinations of the thesis. The hand of
God seems peculiarly present to us : again and
again within but a few months it has pleased Him—
in mercy, we trust, as well as in severity—to strike
down one and another of our foremost men, leaving blanks in families, and gaps in wider circles,
never to be filled up. Surely there is a lesson
in these things ! Surely we are to learn something more from such visitations than a mere cold
reflection upon the uncertainty of life, upon the
miscalculations of self-confidence, or the strange
startling suddenness with which a man may be hur-
ried from amidst the commonplace familiarities of
things temporal into the marvellous, the inscrut-
able mysteries of a world eternal ! If such events
are ever to be turned to their true account, it must
be by a deeper and a more thorough work than
this. If each death occasioned the new birth
but of one soul, it would be worth all the havoc
which it makes of loving and happy homes. Let us
then for this time—our minds sobered and solem-
nized by God's dealing—endeavour so to use the
brief moments of this meditation, as that it may

work in us, through grace, some serious heart-deep resolutions which may bring forth fruit unto life eternal!

The Fugitive seeking Freedom in a far Country.

1. We are going to speak now of God's fugitives. Are we amongst them? I suspect that all of us either are so or have been. The text tells us that even a Prophet may be one of God's fugitives. His very commission (in this case) made him so. That which he ought to have regarded as a great honour laid upon him—to be allowed to do a work for God in calling a wicked place to repentance—is the occasion of bringing out the selfishness and rebellion of his heart, and he rises up to flee to a distant land from the presence of the Lord. It was an ignorant thought, you say. One whom God had brought so nigh to Himself ought to have been able to say, in answer to such a temptation, *Whither shall I go from Thy Spirit? or whither shall I flee from Thy presence? If I ascend up into heaven, Thou art there: if I make my bed in hell, behold, Thou art there. If I take the wings of the morning, and dwell in the uttermost parts of the sea; even there shall Thy hand lead me, and Thy right hand shall hold me.*

And yet, I repeat it, we are all prone to the same error and to the same sin still.

This Prophet fled from a duty. He was to go and cry against Nineveh—and he would not. He feared the peril of such an enterprise—he feared its difficulty—perhaps he feared its ridicule. And thus, rather than obey, he would become one of God's fugitives. Perhaps he might find a shore on which God was not! Perhaps he might escape God's notice, lying in *the sides of the ship*, and rapidly sailing away from the sacrifices and from the sanctuaries of Israel!

And which of us has not known what it is to flee away from an irksome duty? Oh, how many things which ought to be done, do we daily leave undone! All the day long, in one form or another, we are fugitives from our duty. One excuse after another suggests itself for postponing, for evading, for fleeing from, something which we know all the time God has laid upon us to be done. And at certain moments in life—sometimes for long years of life together—we are guilty of more than this common negligence, this ordinary procrastination, of small particulars of duty. Who has not known what it is—yes, some perhaps

have not known, but thousands too well understand it—to avoid, to dread, to hate, some definite
thing which God has appointed him? to refuse to
be reconciled, it may be, to some one whom my
own fault, more than the other's, has estranged?
to refuse to discharge some debt of love or mercy,
which, till it is paid, must lie like a millstone upon
the stiff neck? it may be, to refuse to bear God's
message of warning to some near friend whom we
know to be trifling on the brink of ruin, God's
word of grace and salvation to some loving but
careless soul which without it may be for ever
lost?

These are hints, necessarily vague and general,
as to the possibility of being God's fugitives in reference to some definite call of duty. But the
case is commoner yet, and even more critical, in
which the flight is not from one thing which ought
to be done, but rather, in general, from a holiness
which condemns and from a presence which over-
awes us. The great revelations of sin and salvation, made in the Law and in the Gospel, are no
secrets to any one born in a Christian land and
brought up amongst the ordinances of our holy
faith. Deep down in every conscience there is

an echo to these sounds. We all know that we ought to repent and turn to God, and do works meet for repentance. We all know that we ought to come to God through Jesus Christ, to seek from Him pardon and grace, and to live day by day in preparation for death and judgment. These things are no secrets to any man. There is a voice within, which enforces them : there is a voice within, which bears witness against a life of carelessness, a life of godlessness, a life of worldliness, a life of sin. Perhaps there is scarcely one person amongst us all, who has not at times given heed to these strivings of the Spirit—sought to listen to God's Word, and to open the closed door between himself and his Saviour. Many have lived, for a few days or weeks at a time, under serious impressions, almost persuaded to become Christians indeed. The hand of God is strong and powerful, as it works in the dispensations of His Providence, and seeks to make them minister to the purposes of His grace. Oh, there is no life quite let alone of God from the cradle to the grave ! And certainly I believe there are none amongst us all, whose heart's desire and prayer is not, *Let me die the death of the righteous !* let me not die impenitent ! let me not awake from

the pain of dying, to find myself in torments!
Therefore I say that, so far as knowledge is concerned, and so far as conviction is concerned, and
so far as general intentions and aspirations are
concerned, we all have that in us which responds
to the voice of God in the Gospel.

But are all then obeying that voice? Are none
of us, this very day, fugitives from it? fleeing from
the presence of the Lord, in the very act of seeming to seek it? This too is possible. This is the
very cause why many worship. If they gave up the
forms of religion, the inward voice might become
too loud for them! They might not be able quite
openly to flee from God's presence—they would
be ashamed and afraid to do that. But this outward form of seeking Him—this one Sunday service which lasts them for the week—just keeps
the conscience still, and enables them all the
better to be fugitives from God in heart and life.
These are the tricks and subterfuges of the sinner
—by which alone he makes it possible for himself
to live without God in the world.

2. And what now is the fugitive seeking?

We might describe his object by many names.
We might call it pleasure—or we might call it self-

indulgence—or we might call it rest and repose—
or we might divide it into those more definite departments of self-pleasing, one of which is the lure
of one man and another of another. But at present
we call it by a very comprehensive term, embrac-
ing in itself all the rest: the Fugitive is seeking
Freedom, seeking Liberty.

O much-dishonoured, much-abused name! What
folly, what sin, what crime, what outrage, has not
sheltered itself, at one time or another, under the
sacred title of freedom? We have seen what it
comes to on a large scale; when a nation has set
itself to be free, in the sense of emancipation from
law, emancipation from order, emancipation from
religion, emancipation from God. We have seen
what it came to: what foul and bloodthirsty licence
—what retributive, what mutual, what suicidal
slaughter—till at last the world stepped in to remonstrate, and an iron despotism crushed out
beneath its heel the last spark of independence
and of self-rule! And we have seen too, all of us,
on a very small scale, what the pursuit of liberty
may end in: we have seen a son shaking off the
easy yoke of home-affection, casting behind his
back the safe and blessed privilege of that unbought

and unselfish love, that he may wallow in the mire
of degrading passions, bring shame on his name
and a curse upon her that bare him. We have
seen what this kind of freedom comes to :—and
perhaps in these most horrible forms we should all
of us shrink from and repudiate it. Yet are these
worst excesses and most frightful riots of freedom,
only representative, only typical, of that which
happens every day in the souls of God's fugitives.
What is it which they count freedom? Is it not
the power of pleasing themselves—of doing what
they list—of living by themselves and to themselves
(so far as God is concerned) in an existence which
yet, whether they will or no, is all of His giving
and of His preserving and of His ordering? They
will say, and count it a just and a convincing argument, Our words and thoughts, our habits and
actions, the members of our bodies and the faculties of our minds, all are our own—who is lord
over us? Let us live as we will—none can call us
to account : let us believe or not believe, let us
obey or disobey, let us follow this course or that,
live for this object, or for that, or for no object—
we are independent, we are irresponsible, we will
please ourselves, and we will risk the consequences.

It was just so that the first temptation swept away the loyalty and obedience of the creature. *Ye shall be as gods ;* no longer depending day by day upon the favour and upon the will and upon the power of another : ye shall be your own masters —free to believe, free to will, and free to do, without control from above, and without these servile questionings from within ! God's fugitive is seeking Freedom.

And what does he find? Let the conscience, let the memory, let the experience answer.

Every day that we remain apart from God— every day that we rise and rest without prayer— every day that we ask ourselves not, What is right? but, What is pleasant ?—every day that we indulge ourselves in some evil habit, and yield without brave resistance to idleness and selfishness and forgetfulness of God—every such day some new chain is forged for us and fastened on : every such day the free man finds himself more and more a slave : the slave, not of one from whose thral-dom he can escape—or to whose thraldom if he submits himself, he may still be a freeman within—but the slave of a power whose seat is in the will; whose lash smites upon the very soul,

and whose dungeon is the black hideous darkness
of a self-accusing and a self-tormenting despair!
Of all slaveries the most cruel and the most hopeless is that which sin binds upon the sinner; the
yoke of good long left undone and evil willingly
done; the inability to do that which he would,
the horrible constraint and compulsion to sin on
and die! It is of such a slavery as this that the
Word of God speaks in these well-known passages,
*Verily, verily I say unto you, He that committeth
sin is the slave of sin. . . . Know ye not that to
whom ye yield yourselves slaves to obey, his slaves
ye are to whom ye obey? . . . While they promise
them liberty, they themselves are the slaves of corruption; for of whom a man is overcome, of the same
is he brought in bondage.*

God too would have us seek freedom : but not
of this vile and ruinous kind : not the freedom to
believe a lie : not the freedom to do evil (as the
Prophet says) *with both hands*, and bring on
ourselves swift destruction : not the freedom to
seduce other souls to share our hell, tormented
and tormenting for ever : but that freedom
which is the successful pursuit of happiness—
that freedom which is the power both to will

and to do our own good—that freedom which is Christ's discipleship—that freedom which is God's service.

3. There is yet a third point in this thesis: and with it we conclude. Where does God's fugitive seek his freedom? In the far country. He has taken his journey; he has made his voyage: and it is indeed a long journey—a voyage over vast waters—by which a man gets away from his God: God has so fenced us in with mercies—God has so guarded us with the safe keeping of His love —that it takes time and thought and long scheming to get away from Him: the young conscience is still sensitive—the young heart is still tender— and oftentimes, when we even think that we have escaped, we are surprised again and again, in the dark watches of the night, or in the waking visions of noonday, with an unsought and unwelcome visitant from God's presence, reminding us of Him whom we would forget, and bringing us back, chained and in custody, before the tribunal which we fancied ourselves to have defied.

But yet it can be done. It takes time to harden any man: it is a gradual process, it is a slow process, but we can go through with it if we will: we

can break through one barrier, and then another
barrier, and at last find ourselves to be free : when
we would do evil, it becomes easier to us : when
we would spend a day, and a Sunday, and a whole
week, away from God, we find at last that we can :
yes, we are in the far country now : things which
once frightened us now seem safe : things which
once looked impossible, so wicked were they, we
can now do and never tremble : if there is on
earth a peace of God, there is also a counterfeit
of it, which is the peace of death : we can reach
that state, if we will, through long carelessness and
much sinning: and when we have reached it, we
shall begin to understand what freedom is—the
bad freedom, the devil's freedom—freedom to
think our own thoughts, even when they are blas-
phemous ; freedom to live our own lives, even
when they are wicked ; freedom to work out our
own ruin without much fear and trembling : the
fugitive has sought freedom—he has also found it
—in the far country : God can be kept out of it for
days and months and years : we think we have
triumphed over Him : the thing formed can say
to Him that formed it, I am free—I am my own—
where art Thou?

Then is the work of rebellion perfected : the fugitive is in the far country—and he has found his freedom.

It is not for this time to tell how God comes after him even there ; how the right-aiming thunderbolts can gleam and scare still in that distance; or how even there God can make His name known, and vindicate His supremacy over all the earth.

Even there—even in that far world—even in the fancied triumph of that flight and of that defiance— the heart of Divine love yearns over the fugitive still, and would win him back, while yet there is time, to a better rest and a securer home.

You know that you are not happy. There is something, even there, which says to you, *This is not your rest:* you were born for something better : the husks that the swine eat are not the food of souls : there is a home behind as well as a home above—a home from which you have wandered, a home of which the memories are about you still, a home of which the doors are still open and the tender mercies ever free ! *O Israel, thou hast destroyed thyself: but in me is thy help. . . . O Israel, return: for thou hast fallen by thine iniquity : take with you words, and turn to the Lord:* say, *Father, I have sinned*—and plead earnestly before Him those compassions which are every morning new.

Sleepers, wake! Fugitives, hasten home! Still the Bridegroom tarries: still the doors are open! O wait not till the expiring lamp warns you of your fatal slumber! Wait not till the gate be for ever closed, and they that come afterwards must stand through a dayless night in the chill outer darkness! *He saith, I have heard thee in an accepted time; and in a day of salvation have I succoured thee: Behold, now is the accepted time; behold, now is the day of salvation!*

III

THE REBEL REFUSING TO RECEIVE CORRECTION.

" Thou hast stricken them, . . . but they have refused to
receive correction."—JER. v. 3.

THE Son has become the Fugitive, and
the Fugitive has become the Rebel.

Such is the downward course of the
human being. Now we are to see it at its worst.
May it be with deep compassion, if the case be
not ours—with earnest contrition, if it be !

1. Who is the Rebel?

To rebel is properly to renew warfare. The
conquered cities which for twelve years served
Chedorlaomer, *in the thirteenth year rebelled:* that
is, they renewed the war; reopened the question
of servitude; reasserted their claim to independence, and brought upon themselves a second
struggle and a second conquest.

In this its original meaning the word Rebel is applicable to every sinner.

The war between man and his God was ended once for all when Christ suffered. *God was in Christ reconciling the world unto Himself.* And in that *world* were we—all mankind : all who sinned in Adam were redeemed and reconciled in Christ. We saw in our first subject that we are all sons : sons first by Creation ; then sons by Redemption ; then sons, thirdly, by individual incorporation into the Church and body of Christ. Therefore, whosoever sins, also rebels—renews a finished war, and breaks an established reconciliation.

It is a great matter—lying very near the root of all true religion—to understand and lay hold of this. All mankind were redeemed to God by the blood of Christ : all baptized persons are sons by a special adoption and by an individual incorporation. Every child ought to be brought up, in Christian homes and in Christian schools, on this supposition. He ought to regard himself, and he ought to be treated by others, as verily and indeed a member of Christ, a child of God, and an inheritor of the kingdom of heaven. There is no doubt that he is inside the home : there is no

S

reason why he should ever quit it. Peace with God, a willing obedience, a loving service—these things ought to be his from the very first: they are so, by God's gift—they are so, by God's will: if they are not so on his part, not so by a glad acceptance and by a cheerful devotion, the fault is his only: the son has fretted against the restraints of his home, till at last he has even become a fugitive seeking rest in a far country: the sinner is not obliged to sin; if he will sin, he is not continuing a war but rather breaking a peace; rising against the loving hand which rules but to bless: in the original sense of the word rebel—the renewer of a once finished war—the sinner is always a rebel too.

But we use the word now in a somewhat different and more popular sense. We use it as expressing a state beyond that of a discontented son, beyond that of an insubordinate exile. It is the third and lowest step on the ladder of the self-ruin. It corresponds to that particular section of the Parable of the Prodigal Son, in which the young man, having demanded his portion, and having carried it with him into the far country, and having wasted it for some time in riotous living, has at last begun to feel the discipline of degradation and wretchedness, the leanness of that dreadful soul-famine, and the grovelling for a morsel of food amongst the husks that the very swine did eat. The word rebel is chosen to express this lowest depth of the sinner's ruin.

Let us look into it a little. And that not coldly, not as idle bystanders, not as curious spectators —but as persons deeply interested; as having in ourselves the germs and elements (at least) of this and of every evil thing ; many of us as more than this—as being now, or as having once been, ourselves sunk and lost in this sea of distress and despair.

The rebel spoken of is, of course, in general terms, a rebel against his God. He has taken up arms in that hopeless, that unnatural strife, which the fallen mortal creature is waging, for his brief day, against Him who formed him. He is *striving* (as the Prophet says) *with his Maker.*

Does this expression sound exaggerated to any one? Do these seem to be hard terms to apply to a life which bears so few outward marks perhaps of being a struggle against any one—which seems rather to have its chief mark, its principal fault, just in being too easy, too little of a conflict, too much a mere letting alone, or a mere floating down life's stream, taking things as they come, and obeying impulses without doubt or questioning?

Then let us examine two or three points in this rebellion. We are speaking of one who has already left God's home; of one who is already in the far country: living, that is, from day to day without thinking upon God; going to his daily labour without prayer; doing what he likes to do, or what he is tempted to do, without asking himself, Is this right? is this consistent with duty? is this the will of God? Of such a man we say, first of all, that—

He is a rebel against light.

It is easy to say that men have different standards, judge variously of right and wrong, count a certain pleasure or a certain gain innocent or unlawful according to early instructions, long associations, rooted habits of thought and action, in which no two persons are exactly alike. Doubtless in smaller particulars this is true. Let no man judge another—let no man even judge for another—in such matters. But the rebel, the man who is living without God day by day, can shelter himself under no such excuses. As to the great broad outlines there is no difference of judgment. One man knows as well as another what is a sin. God leaves no one without witness. There is that in each bosom which gives its name, of right or wrong, to each separate thing that we do or leave undone. And that inward tribunal we carry with us even into the far country. We cannot put it down; we cannot leave it behind. However disregarded, however despised, however outraged, that inward judge speaks and will speak, and so makes the sinner against God a rebel also, in the first place, against light.

He is a rebel also against power.

We think it a mark of great infatuation, when a thoroughly vanquished and prostrate race will periodically renew its impotent rebellion against the giant empire which holds it down. But how faint and poor an image is this kind of idle struggling, in comparison with that which a sinner undertakes against his God! In Him we live and move and have our being. It is He who gives the man of business *power to get wealth:* it is He who endowed the eloquent tongue with its speech, and the inventive brain with its cunning: it is He who nightly refreshes with sleep, and daily renews with waking: *when He taketh away our breath, we die, and are turned again to our dust.* Therefore when we do the thing which we know God disapproves, when we try to dispense with that prayer which is the soul's exercise and air and daily bread, how can we even expect it to end well? There must come a time when sin shall be seen by us to have been exceeding sinful; when that evil thing which we would try to call good shall find us out at last in remorse and punishment.

And we see the guilt and the folly yet more plainly, when we add this—that the rebel against God is a rebel against love.

The word ungrateful has a harsh sound, a condemning sense, as between a man and his fellow. To tell of benefits on one side unsparingly lavished, and on the other side unthankfully enjoyed, is to raise in our fallen nature a feeling of righteous indignation. It is not a question of religion, whether an undutiful son, whether a trusted and untrustworthy servant, whether an outcast youth raised from indigence and refusing to acknowledge and bless his benefactor, is worthy of respect or of abhorrence: we all feel it as we ought in human life : how is it that we do not feel it as between man and God? Everything that we have is of God ; everything that God commands He commands not for His good but for ours ; every call which He sends He sends to draw us towards happiness ; everything which He requires He recompenses as though it were some meritorious service : and if then we sin, we are shutting out love ; if we are disobedient, we are ungrateful too ; if we are living in vanity, in ungodliness, in sin, we are not only rebels against light, and rebels against power ; we are this also, beyond and above all else—rebels against love.

2. But now observe, as the text and the subject bid us, that even this rebel is not let alone.

Men are apt to say—some men have said it in words, and many more say it in their thoughts—*God has long ago given me up.* And it cannot be denied—we all want the painful truth for warning and for quickening—that there are some passages of Holy Scripture which seem to tell of a hardening, even in this life, not only inveterate but judicial; of *a sin unto death* for which prayer itself may rise in vain from a brother. But even these solemn words are not to be so applied by any man as to

form a reason why he personally should not
struggle, should not pray, should not hope. If he
but desires to do any one of these things, he may
be sure that he has not yet committed (be it what
it may) the unpardonable offence. And speaking
generally, and of that which alone any of us can
know, we may say with confidence that even
towards the most rebellious God is still using a
discipline which is here called correction. It is
the word which especially denotes the correction
of a child by his father. It is the word used, for
example, in that well-known saying of the Book of
Proverbs, *Foolishness is bound in the heart of a child;
but the rod of correction shall drive it far from him.*
And so, in its transfer (as here) to God's discipline, we read in the Book of Job, *Behold, happy
is the man whom God correcteth: therefore despise
not thou the chastening (correction) of the Almighty.*
It is not so much in the treatment—it is rather in
his use of the treatment—that man differs from
man, the rebel from the Christian, during his trial
and probation-time below. *Thou hast stricken
them—but they have refused to receive correction.*

The hand of God is far-reaching. It is not only
in the home of the son, it is not only within the

Paradise of the upright, it is also over the remote exile, over the wilful wanderer, over the obstinate rebel, that that *hand is stretched out still*, for correction, for control—if he will, for blessing. So long as we live, God is dealing with us : we cannot get away from His presence ; we cannot really make our escape from His Spirit.

It is a serious thought—full of admonition—surely for each one of us full of encouragement.

What a key is here to the mysteries of our being ! This strange scene, this tangled web, this clueless labyrinth, of chance and change, of success and defeat, of enjoyment and suffering, of tranquillity and desolation, which human life presents on the surface, and which seems to a careless looker-on as though nothing and no one could explain it—yet, if this word correction has any meaning, if the term discipline has any application to these matters, the riddle is more than half read. If the hand which holds the thread of destiny, if the power which besets and begirds us all round, and out of which there is evidently no escape for any one, is a hand of wise counsel and a power of loving forethought—a hand which works towards an end, and a power which is not so much force as rule—if this be so, then not only can we trust where we see not, but even in the thickest darkness there arises upon us at once a marvellous light.

There is no thought more wonderfully compounded of mercy and judgment, than that of God's correction as exercised towards His rebels. *Yea, for the rebellious also*, says the Psalmist, *that the Lord God might dwell among them.* That is the end in view: not, as some would say, for greater condemnation ; not, as theorists might put it, to stop the mouth of cavil, and deprive guilt itself of its last excuse; not thus—but with the desire—say it reverently, but say it still—with the desire that the closed heart may at last open itself, and the hard frozen spirit thaw and melt, ere it be too late, under the sunbeam of the Divine love. *Yea, for the rebellious also, that the Lord God might dwell among them.*

Sometimes we draw into detail the working of this correction. It is exercised in all manner of ways. The resources of the Creator are of course absolutely infinite. He who made man's heart— He who in the beginning arranged within us the whole mechanism of feeling and motive, of influence and impulse, of thought and affection, of desire, resolution, and will—can bring to bear upon each just that touch which shall be persuasive; can apply, with a skill as true as the power is resistless, circumstances to dispositions, and means to ends, outward things to things inward, and natural agencies to spiritual conditions; insomuch that eternity shall not exhaust the retrospect of lives carefully guided through the world's wilderness, and souls marvellously disciplined into a capacity and receptivity of grace.

All these operations are far above out of our sight. *Such knowledge is too wonderful and excellent for us: we cannot attain to it.* Nevertheless, in the belief that God is working—working in a Providence as minute as it is universal, and as considerate as it is resistless; working everywhere and in all things, for man's discipline and correction in righteousness—in the belief of these things, strongly grasped and tenaciously clung to, lies the only rest for troubled thoughts, the only satisfaction for interminable doubtings; even in the assurance that God has not deserted His earth, but is guiding all His counsels towards a goal of perfect happiness and perfect love.

3. But for the present we are to dwell upon the use made by the rebellious of the Divine discipline. *Thou hast stricken them—but they have refused to receive correction.* The correction is there, not for all only, but for each; only the rebel refuses to receive it.

It may be the outward correction: that which comes to a man in Providential circumstances: the correction of loss and disappointment, the correction of failure and loneliness, the correction of sorrow and bereavement, of diminished strength, waning comfort, supports withdrawn, and shattered idols.

It may be that correction which lies in the direct consequences and punishments of sin: the paralyzed frame, witnessing in mid life to youth's excesses; the shame which follows upon certain discoveries; the destruction of earth's prospect with the departure of earth's respect: it may be even the felon's prison and the condemned man's cell. These too, if they be but so taken, are God's corrections for His rebels: even out of these, through the wondrous working of Divine grace, there have sprung, as of old for the penitent malefactor on Calvary, words of precious absolution, promises of a Paradise that very day opened, and a remembrance, late sought but sure, in the coming of the Saviour's kingdom.

Or it may be, once again, an entirely inward correction : as when some particular sin lies with crushing weight upon the conscience; when the thought of a brother's injured soul comes back as a torturer and an executioner in the night's endless watches; when the vivid sense of ingratitude and heartlessness, towards man or towards God, flashes a scaring searing light upon the transgressor, and in the hopeless consciousness of irreparable evil he feels hell itself opened, and the frightful endless torment before its due time begun.

Less things than these : a mighty famine arising upon the wanderer who has already spent his all; a deep unutterable sense of vacuity, desolation, and nothingness, even while life still smiles, and the fortune of the self-tormentor is the envy of a beholding world. And this there may be, where there has been little perhaps of open, gross, notorious sin ; where no brother's blood, of ruined life or lost soul, cries from the ground for vengeance ; where there has been much that is amiable and nothing that is disgraceful—only a world too much lived for, and a God of grace and redemption banished from all the thoughts.

Now it is the nature of the rebel to refuse to receive these corrections. We will say just two things.

First, he misunderstands them.

For a long time he does not connect them at all with the thought of God. He calls them misfortunes—calamities—hardships—incalculable disappointments of his reckoning—things which fall upon him when they fall not upon this man and that man of his acquaintance who had done just the same—injuries therefore and injustices of fortune, rather than the due requitals of a wrong and wicked and Godless course of life.

This of the outward corrections. And then for the inward. That aching void, that miserable consciousness of a purposeless wasted life, that keen self-reproach for definite sins, or that scarcely less keen self-reproach for an utterly useless, selfish, God-forgetting existence—all this he calls weakness, low spirits, melancholy, unaccountable depression, due more to the health than to the soul; something that must be shaken off by changes of air and scene; something that must be charmed

away by cheerful converse, or exorcised by a resolute and vigorous self-control.

Thus he misunderstands his symptoms, by sever-
ing them, while he can, from any connexion with
the conscience or with the hand of God.

And when this cannot be; when the arrow
fastens itself too deeply and too unmistakably
within to leave room for doubt whence it comes,
whose hand forged and whose bow discharged it;
then the misunderstanding of the Author changes
into a misconception of the motive. Then the man
says, Not because God loved me and would save,
but because He hated and would destroy, is this
misery come upon me: let me alone, that I may
hopelessly suffer: let me alone, that I may curse
God and die. It is no imaginary reasoning which
we thus describe: thousands of thousands amongst
God's fallen creatures have thus set and steeled
themselves against the fatherly hand, when it in-
terposed at last to bring sin to remembrance, not
that it should be clung to and perished with, but
that it should be shaken off, cast away, and fled
from. The hand was the hand of love: only the
life on which it was laid was the life of one who
would not be loved.

Then, finally, he who has misunderstood the correction, goes on to neutralize it.

This too is possible.   This too is easy.

A man who ought to be much alone with his sorrow, will rush out into the world to get rid of it.   A man who ought to enter very deeply into the why and the wherefore of correction; taking himself to task, and sitting in judgment upon himself, to know for what reason God is contending with him; will go anywhere to have his hurt healed slightly; to be made to think that the affliction has no meaning, or not this; to be assured by sympathizing friends that he has no cause for uneasiness; that, in this case at least, *trouble has sprung out of the ground*, and that it brings with it therefore for him neither reproof nor doctrine. The consequence is that he too *refuses to receive correction*, neutralizing its gracious import by a slight and superficial treatment.

And thus it may go on even to the end.   Even old age may come—as the Prophet says, *gray hairs are here and there upon him, yet he knoweth not*— knoweth not the sign of an approaching end, knoweth not nor considereth the day of his visitation.   It is so, often, even on a death-bed: to the very last day, the hand of correction is unnoticed, and he who has lived in thoughtlessness and worldliness will rush unprepared to meet his God!

I would not willingly call any one here present a rebel (in this sense) against his God. Yet even in the congregation there are hearts knowing their own bitterness; yea, hearts writing bitter things against themselves by reason of conscious unfaithfulness, and long and obstinate alienation from God. And of these, and of all, I would make one last request: that they would try themselves by this one criterion—their behaviour towards God's corrections: feeling well assured that His corrections are abroad amongst us, and that great and sore is the peril of their being either misconstrued or misused. Let it not be said of us that we either despised God's chastening, or (on the other hand) fainted under His correction; that we either slighted as an unmeaning thing, or resented as an unkind thing, that breach in the even tenor of an unbroken prosperity, by which God both reminds us of His reality and seeks to draw us towards His repose. *He who spared not His own Son* may well see suffering to be the necessity of His people.

T

He who raised up the Lord Jesus will both manifest the risen life of Jesus in the mortal flesh and in the trying fortunes of His people, and at last *raise them also by Jesus,* and *present them faultless before the presence of His glory.*

IV.

COMPUNCTIOUS VISITINGS AND REPENTANT RESOLUTIONS.

"I have surely heard Ephraim bemoaning himself thus."
—JER. xxxi. 18.

HE story of a life—the whole story of a whole life—what a marvel! what a mystery! Who can write it, save One alone?

Well can we understand that such a record should have, as our Lord instructs us, an interest even in heaven. If it is given to those ministering spirits who behold the face of God, to track the course of a soul; to follow the wanderings, and read the riddles, and unravel the complications, of one single real life, as it forms its own character, and works out its own destiny, on this little stage of present being; well may it be that they should find in such contemplations a deep, an almost absorbing interest; that they should wonder and vex themselves, that they should even suffer and weep, over the perversenesses of these rebels against grace and redemption : and if, in one case and another, under this influence or that, they discern at last a decisive return from long wanderings, a true repentance and reformation in one who has hitherto set himself to oppose and counteract God's correction, that then the words should be verified which were spoken once on earth by our Lord Jesus Christ, *Joy shall be in heaven over one sinner that repenteth, more than over ninety and nine just persons, which need no repentance.*

God grant to each of us some portion of the same sympathy, the same yearning over tempted and imperilled and battling souls, as we ponder at this time the subject proposed to us—those *compunctious visitings and repentant resolutions* which have formed in all ages, for so many thousands of our fallen race, the very turning-point and transition from the death of sin to the life of righteousness !

I trust that the past week has witnessed amongst ourselves some of these workings of Divine grace. I trust that this very night will seal some of these vows unchangeably at the table of Christ's dying love. That so the army of the faithful may be replenished in this place with new soldiers, and the joy of heaven refreshed and rekindled by the spectacle of a great repentance.

We have dwelt hitherto upon the dark side of the soul's life. We have seen the son becoming the fugitive, and the fugitive hardening into the rebel. We have seen the original love thanklessly slighted, and the patient correction obstinately refused. In all this we have had only to go into the heart for its experiences, and pour them forth into other hearts similarly exercised. How shall it be now? Must we part company at this point, and speak of things which all but a few know not? Oh, not so, my brethren! Even now let us go all together, and seek Him from whom in different ways and degrees all have wandered!

1. I will not then enter now into what we may call the more exceptional regrets and remorses of sinful souls. I will not speak of definite acts of cruel wrong done to others, nor of such impieties towards God as but one here and there can have been guilty of. Our Lord touches a different and a more thrilling chord, when He makes the wanderer, in his uttermost destitution, think of the

plenty of his home; compare what he might have been with what he is, and say, as he comes to himself, only just this, *How many hired servants of my father's have bread enough and to spare, and I perish with hunger!*

And so now, this evening, in the few moments left to us by the coming Service, let us lay this one thought to heart—how good and blessed a thing it is to be even anywhere, even in the lowest and meanest place, within the true house and home of God; how evil and bitter a thing to have ever left it, to have wandered away into the far country for the sake of being rid of those restraints, which are themselves, for all who will view them aright, no chain of bondage, but rather a perfected freedom.

This is the *compunction* which I would have to *visit* us. I would have the undutiful son, I would have the wilful wayward exile, I would have the hardened rebel, say to himself this night, Would that I had never left my home! God Himself was my Father: He created, He redeemed, He called me: He set me within His doors, by no choice of mine, when I was a dumb senseless infant: He provided for my training in Christian knowledge, He gave me ordinances of worship, He put His Word in my hand, He caused me to know right from wrong, the way of salvation from the way of ruin : all this He did for me, and I would none of Him. Day after day, as I grew up, I relaxed a little, and yet a little more, of my known rule of duty : I began to give up praying, I trifled with His sacred day, I counted worship a burden, I cared not to give thanks, I thought forgetfulness pleasure, and self-indulgence happiness : thus I lived : not without occasional reminiscences of better things ; not without some strivings of conscience, not without some faint short-lived endeavours after righteousness ; but still, on the whole, away from God, at a distance from God, *without God in the world.*

And now I am reaping the fruits of this. There is a great famine within me ; *not of bread nor of water*, as the Prophet writes, but of God's Word, of God's presence, of comfort and peace, of rest and hope. When trouble comes, *I have no place to flee unto :* when I would weep, my heart is a stone : when death strikes down another beside me, though I tremble I cannot feel ; cannot feel, that is, as I ought, the lesson God would teach, nor learn so to number my own days as to apply my heart to wisdom. And when I am in prosperity, God is not in all my thoughts : I live for the hour and for the day, I live not for God and the soul, for Christ and eternity. Oh, I am very far from God—I who, by right and title at least, was once within the home.

And now something brings to me just the wish, just the sigh, after something better. I look perhaps upon one beside me, who is different : different just in this one point : not in being higher than I in outward advantage ; not in being richer, or nobler, or more successful ; it may be, quite the contrary—poor, while I am rich ; disappointed, while I am prosperous ; a servant, perhaps, while I am a master—inferior, then, in all these things— but in one thing above me ; that he is inside the home ; that he has never left, or has long returned to, the family of God ; that he knows in whom he believes, and is persuaded that He can keep, and will keep, against the day of Christ, the deposit of his life and of his soul.   I see him, just because he is inside that home, with *bread enough and to spare :* always contented, always satisfied, always thankful ; ingenious (as man might say) in seeing only

good, seeing mercy in severity and love in suffering; never doubting the gracious purpose, and
never harbouring a mistrust of the wisdom which
is guiding all things towards an end. *Bread enough
and to spare—and I perish with hunger*—I, a
child—I, a son!

There are young people in this congregation—
God grant there may be elder persons too—whose
hearts are in this frame this evening. They are
reproaching themselves, not for this crime or that;
not so much for this or that which they have
done or left undone; but rather with the waste of
blessing, with the general refusal of love, of which
they have been guilty; with having left God's
home; with having forsaken *the Guide of their
youth;* with having dealt unthankfully and heart-
lessly with Him who was never weary of doing
them good. And now they would return—did
they but know the way—could they but be sure of
being let in!

This is the true compunction—that *pricking
of the heart,* of which Scripture tells: not the
panic terror of one before whose eyes hell has
suddenly opened herself; not the abject cringing
fear of Divine vengeance, which with many is the

beginning, middle, and end too, of all conversion : no, the returning thought of home ; the recollection of a Divine family and household of which I was by inheritance and adoption a member ; the recollection of a Divine name and face and relationship which I still designate as that of a Father ; the coming back upon me of a something, of a some One, kinder and more lovely and more desirable than all the vain things for which I have sacrificed it ; the reminiscence of a bright and ordered dwelling, in which the very menials were princes—and the deep inner questioning, Why am I absent now from that dwelling ? who shall restore me—or is it too late—to that home of my infancy which still casts its light upon me from afar in my wretchedness and in my exile ?

I pause for one moment to say to those in this place who are already inmates of the Divine home, See that you make it desirable, to them that are without ! See that they be constrained to say of you, He the servant, she the handmaid, of that home, has evidently enough and to spare ! Let it be seen of all that you are happy, that you are at peace, that you are satisfied, contented, restful, hopeful ! It is thus that souls are drawn to Jesus ;

by the sight of that peace, of that happiness, which He communicates. It is thus that compunctions visit exiled sons ; through the bright blessed faces of those who have found rest in Christ.

2. This is that Compunction of which we would speak. And now of the Resolution.

We have called it a repentant resolution : hoping that you would all understand by *repentant*, not gloomy, not remorseful, not black and blank and despairing, but that which it indeed is, *of* or *belonging to a changed mind*, to a new mind, the mind which sees all things in an altered light— sin as exceeding sinful, and holiness as altogether blessed.

Repentant Resolutions.

I will arise, and go to my Father—and will say unto Him, Father—I have sinned against heaven and before Thee—against Thee, and in the sight of heaven.

Mark first how the repentant resolution speaks of God. *My Father.*

Yes, you may have sinned ; you may have gone a long way in sin ; you may have cast behind your back Christian habits—habits of prayer, of wor-

ship, of religious observance, even of moral duty—
yet are you a Son still; and your God is your
Father still!

Happy is he—God grant us grace to make the
thought more present to any one!—who in his
remotest exile, in his uttermost destitution, still
speaks, still thinks, of God as his Father.

That relation can never be lost—not while life
lasts; we say not how it may be hereafter!

Say to yourself, God is my Father. That is my
chief sin, that I left Him being such; that, though
He is my Father, and though His presence is therefore my home, yet I left Him; ran away from Him;
entered the devil's service; tried to make him my
Father instead of God.

But I could not. The moment that the thought
comes back to me, *God is my rightful owner, and
God my rightful Lord*, that moment the relation
springs again into fullest force, *God is thy Father
too!*

Again, *I will arise.*

Yes, there is need of exertion. Sit still, and
thou art bound; sorry, but not contrite; miserable,
but not repentant. *I will arise*, must the soul say:
I will shake off the lethargy: I will break the fetter

of sleep and indolence : *I will arise and go :* there is a journey, though it be but in the soul's going ; and therefore there must be a rising, a rousing of the whole man, like that which in the days of the Son of God below enabled one whose hand was withered, yet at the Divine command to stand forth and stretch it out.

The power is given in the willing. Say, *I will arise,* and grace shall lift thee up.

And *I will go.* Whither, and how ?

First, in prayer. We have called it a soul's journey. The soul must arise and pray. As if God were present—knowing that God is present—because God is present—so, and thus, and therefore, speak to Him. Say, *Father, I have sinned—* say it—He hears !

Oh the marvellous power of that little commonplace thing which we call prayer ! So soon done ; so often supposed to be done by every man ; so often not done when it has been (by a reckoning of time) even long and earnest ! Yet, where the will once is, done almost in no time ; done (it may be) without word or sound or sign ; done in the heart of the man ; done in the ear of his God !

I will arise, and I will go, and I will say, Father,

I have sinned! Say that, from the heart, as to a present and a prayer-hearing God—and the work is done !

And again, Go, in effort. We must not trifle with or mock God : and therefore he who would pray must endeavour too. In particular, we must resolutely give up known sins. We are all such cowards : cowards with ourselves : we dare not say within, *I will,* and *I will not :* we yield up the helm to chance, to habit, to temptation—to something not to be called temptation—mere idleness, indolence, or what not. If we would only pray first, and then try, we could do so many things, and forbear so many : but we are cowards, the best of us, towards our own poor selves. Cowards too towards the devil, and towards his agents and tools around. *Resist the devil,* St James says, *and he will flee from you :* for he too is a coward, and the chief of cowards ; bold towards the timid, dastardly before the brave. Therefore, I say, he who would arise and go—and this is the repentant resolution of which alone we speak to-night—must face his own sins, his own chief sin, in the name of Christ ; face it, and beat it too ! Let it not be, that we should be resolute and brave in all else,

and yet cowards and dastards towards that which
is our one foe! *Give up your sin,* is the first
word of Christ to those who would return to their
Father.

And then, thirdly and lastly, Go, in the use of all
means. God has furnished us with various means
and instruments of access to Him. Such is His
Holy Word, read and pondered daily and prayed
over. Such are all those occasions of Christian
converse, in which *they who fear the Lord speak
one to another,* for mutual edification and strengthening, *and the Lord hearkens,* and opens for them
His blessed book of everlasting remembrance.
One such is that to which you have heard yourselves bidden to-day; a weekly meeting, under
the guidance of an appointed Minister, for reading,
for instruction, for praise, for prayer. Such, above
all, is that ordinance of Divine Communion to
which—so many of us for the first time—we are
all invited this evening. Be not backward thus to
arise and go to your Father! He is very present
at that Table. There, more than anywhere below, He flings back the folding-gates of His house,
and bids the erring son to enter. Say not in your
hearts, any one, Thus far will I follow, but I will

not go in : I came to Confirmation, but I come not
to Communion.   Weigh not out thus your service
by grains and scruples !   If Confirmation meant
anything, it meant Communion.   He who could
say with a clear conscience last Friday, *I do*,
can say this evening, *I come.*   Neither the one
nor the other are professions of attainment : both
the one and the other are confessions of need.

I will arise and go to my Father.

We must get to Him somehow.   If we do not
get to God Himself, we have done nothing after
all.   Even public worship, even Holy Communion,
even private prayer and study of the Scriptures,
may stop short of reaching God.   O most unhappy
of all disappointments ! to have done so much, and
yet not attained—to have drawn so near the gate,
and yet never entered !   Therefore we must bear
this in mind, amidst and above all else, that things
which God instituted as means must never be
treated as if they were ends ; in other words, that
we must press through all outward ordinances, as
through so many courtyards and vestibules, into
the actual presence-chamber and shrine of the
Divine Father Himself.   Nothing less, nothing
else, will ever satisfy the immortal man : that,

that alone, is the bread of life; that bread **of** which the very doorkeeper inside the Home has enough and to spare. *Jesus said unto them, I, I myself*—not my ordinances, not my Word, not my Church, not my Supper—I myself—*am the bread of life: he that cometh to me shall never hunger ; and he that believeth on me shall never thirst.*

Lord, evermore give us this bread!

V

THE WANDERER'S WELCOME, AND THE HOME-LIFE OF THE RESTORED.

"They shall be satisfied with the plenteousness of thy house."—PSALM xxxvi. 8.

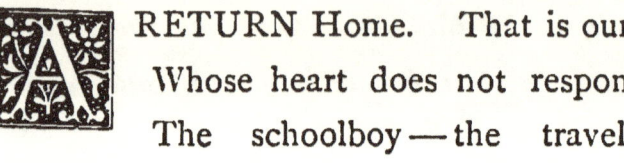RETURN Home. That is our subject. Whose heart does not respond to it? The schoolboy — the traveller — the soldier son—the Indian husband—it is an experience at once among the commonest and among the most memorable; familiar to all, and yet to none trivial; old in itself and in the general, and yet in the feeling and in the instance evermore new likewise.

These are the things which Scripture speaks of; stirring the depths of universal nature into sparkling waves of spiritual influence. Scripture—and He who speaks in Scripture—goes into humanity itself for its illustrations of things Divine. And for this amongst other reasons Scripture is a book for all men ; not for the rich and wise only, nor yet (on the other hand) for the poor and simple only, but for all alike and equally ; because it deals not with the artificialities which overcrust the life of man, but with those matters in which the life itself consists ; speaking a language which all understand, and addressing a soul which all possess.

A Return Home. If that is the figure employed, certainly it is intelligible.

But how is it as to the use, as to the application, of the figure ? Is that also universally appropriate ?

It is a common, and not unnatural feeling, which makes a sinful person isolate himself in his sinfulness. It is one of the strongest barriers which men erect against their own salvation, this argument—My case is peculiar: no one ever sinned quite like me : no one has wandered so far, or so obstinately, or in this particular direction : no one therefore can understand my case, and no one's recovery is any warrant for my hope. Thus secrets are locked up, which ought to be confided to the physician ; and the entrance of God's light into the life and into the soul is rendered impossible, by the determination of the sufferer to regard himself as alone in his guilt, alone in his ruin.

How different the view of Christ!

Evidently He who knows what is in man sees in those whom He came to save a substantial uniformity amidst every possible variety of circumstance. As all need their daily bread, so all need to be forgiven for daily sins. The two petitions follow each other in the Lord's Prayer. And thus, when He tells the story of a life's wandering and a soul's return, He speaks of that which all will understand, and of which all the saved will have had a true experience.

The saints of old time used words of utter self-condemnation when they poured out their soul's secrets in the ear of God. And we in like manner, framing our prayers for universal worship—framing them for worshippers of all sorts and of all histories, and desiring surely that they should express nothing but that which is true in the sight of the Lord—have made this the very language of the Church in her morning and evening devotions through the week and the year and the generation, *Almighty and most merciful Father, we have erred and strayed from thy ways—like lost sheep.*

Now, if this be true, how precious to each one of us ought to be this present subject, the Wanderer's Welcome! We may speak upon it to all— for all, more or less, are Wanderers. We say it ourselves. We have said it of ourselves again and again—we have said it now—*We have erred and strayed.* It is not the excepted case: it is universal. Would to God that we all and each felt it so! For, *if we say that we have not sinned, the truth is not in us—we deceive ourselves!*

The difference is not there: not in the wandering—though the ways in which we have lost ourselves are as various as the thoughts of man's heart — not in the wandering, but in the return.

Some of us have not yet tasted the bitterness of the wandering. The mighty famine has not yet come to us. We have not yet quite run through our portion of goods. Life is but a little way spent: youth, health, strength, spirits, these are still ours: hope is larger than regret, faults are not yet seen as sins, God is not in our thoughts— or, if He comes there at all, it is not as a Person, not as a Life, a Voice, a Power, but only as a name—why should we return? we are but just free; beginning to taste the delicious fruit which is to make us gods : why should we return ?

And others of us, though the famine has arisen, and we are in want, yet cannot make up our minds quite to return : we will try a compromise first : there is a citizen of the country who will employ and feed me : I am not at my last resource yet : that dull distant Home is not yet my only refuge : presently perhaps—in the very end of life—not now, not to-day !

And others have even tried to return, and could not find the way. They had no confidence in the welcome. They could not offer a whole heart. They set out—again and again they set out—but they were hindered—they desponded—they looked behind them—they never arrived. The remembrance of a long succession of half-repentances lies heavy upon them, clogging their steps, and enfeebling effort by destroying hope.

Such are some of the conditions upon which God our Father looks down to-night in this congregation, and still mercifully speaks, even to these, of the Wanderer's Welcome.

How and where is the welcome given ?

What is meant by the Father seeing the erring

son a great way off, and running forth to fall on
his neck and kiss him ?   It is there in the Book—
what is it in fact and in the life ?   How does God
make good the words now ?   By what signs shall
we know, any one of us, that we personally are
welcomed home ?

A deeply important, a deeply solemn question.
I would answer it as simply and seriously as possible.

Many persons build everything upon feeling.
One says, I feel that I am forgiven.   Something
within tells me that I am forgiven.   On such a
day, in such a place, the assurance came to me :
I build upon that.   And another says, I cannot
feel that I am forgiven.   I cannot get peace.   I
was told that I should have an inward sense of
pardon : and I have not got it.   Therefore I am
not yet forgiven.

There must be something a little wrong here.
This sort of doctrine scarcely has the stamp of
truth upon it.   I am forgiven, because I feel that
I am forgiven—I am not forgiven, because I cannot feel that I am forgiven ! that is not like Christ's
teaching : that is not the firm rock of a Gospel, of
a Revelation, of a message brought to us from

God, if, after all, my feeling this or that is to make this or that true, and my not feeling it is to make this or that (which is nothing less than my salvation) false and void !

Well may we pray the Psalmist's prayer, *O set me upon the rock that is higher than I !* This rock, of mere feeling, is not higher than I : it is more precarious, more shifting, more fleeting, even than I : for it takes in but one part of me, and that the least stable and the least stedfast.

We must begin quite differently. The welcome spoken of is, first of all, the sure word of God. Christ *is the Propitiation for our sins, and not for ours only, but also for the sins of the whole world*— that is my welcome home ! Whether I come or come not, Christ bore my sins : it is done ! Let me come, not to get it done, but because it is done ! Let me come, because there is nothing in the way ; because, when I was far off, the Father had compassion, and conveyed to me the tidings of my forgiveness and of my welcome !

And so then, even if I cannot feel it as I would ; even if I still walk in much gloom and in much despondency and in much self-misgiving ; that does not shake the fact : God welcomes me for all that, if I just cling to the drowning man's rope, which is the Cross of Christ !

And when once the matter is taken out of the province of feeling, and carried into the region of simple Revelation, there is this result also—it is one of the proofs of the Divine harmony of the Gospel—that the very refusal to depend upon feeling brings the feeling; that, just in proportion as I look out of myself to Christ alone, take God at His word, and exclude self from my view, in the same proportion peace comes ; not to be trusted in, yet surely to be given thanks for ; not conveying, yet echoing, the welcome ; not making me a son, but yet helping to bear the witness that I am a son of God.

Let a man try this counsel ; let him earnestly pray to God on the strength of the Gospel—coming to Him as a sinner, spreading before Him his exact state, keeping back nothing, treating Him as a Father, from whom he has wandered, but who desires and has provided for his salvation—and let him see whether in the very act he does not also feel a welcome ; whether, as of old, when in days of childhood he confessed some little fault to his father or his mother, and felt himself forgiven, so now, telling out his deeper, graver, viler sins to a Father who seeth in secret, there be not sent into his soul that blessed ray which is the glory of the Divine presence, assuring him of God's hearing, and breathing into his soul, there and then, some answer of peace.

I trust and believe that there are those here present, who are now rejoicing in the Wanderer's Welcome. They have become conscious of sin. They have made a great exertion to shake off the yoke. They have earnestly tried to draw nigh to God. They have set themselves to lay hold on the hope set before them. They have got this night a glimmering at least of hope. Home shines beyond—yea, they are at its door! The Father has compassion, and meets them a long way off with His blessed welcome. Let them take it, and doubt not! It is a free welcome, unfettered by condition or compact—*Whosoever will, let him take the water of life freely!*

But now we are to suppose this first step taken. The return is accomplished. The wanderer is welcomed home. There is joy in heaven over the repenting sinner: joy too on earth in the heart which has found a Father.

Is all done? May we rest here, or float henceforth down a peaceful stream into a safe and
blessed haven?

Some have so learned Christ. They have made
Conversion everything. They have left out of
view all those Scriptures which speak to true con-
verts of working out salvation, of the danger of
falling away, of the daily necessity of faith and
patience, of prayer and watching. Like some old-
fashioned tale, ending with the marriage; stopping
short of the most eventful days, and excluding
from the view the most real trials, of human life;
so does this one-sided doctrine terribly distort the
true estimate of the spiritual being, and stunt the
growth in grace of many who have even entered
upon the true life of Christ.

Therefore it is that we have added now to *the
Wanderer's Welcome* this second thesis also—*and
the Home-life of the Restored.*

Sometimes, in human life, a son returns home,
and will not stay at home. Again, as of old, he
frets against its restraints, and becomes again an
exile. Not for lack of a kindly loving welcome.
Not on account of reproaches for the past, or of
harsh conditions imposed for the future. No, for

the old reason : because the abode of love is un-lovely to the unloving ; because the heart of sin cannot abide in the dwelling of the righteous ; because (as the Prophet says) *two cannot walk together except they be agreed,* and the self-will which has seen the world and tasted of its lawless indulgences can scarcely settle itself down amidst calm unexciting comforts and sober monotonous occupations. The son again becomes the fugi-tive, and the fugitive again hardens into the rebel.

It is so in the case of God's Home. Who has not known, at some time or other of his life, some-thing which may fitly be called a return and a welcome? Of whom has it not now and then been said, and with truth, by his friends, He has turned over a new leaf—he is going on better? Of whom even this, He is sorry for his sin, and is becoming more serious? Who has not, whether observed or unnoticed, at some time or other of his life, made his humble supplication to God for pardon and salvation? That was, if it was sincere, a return home : and at the time how could we doubt the welcome? Yet over and over again in a man's life these things come and go : these changes of feeling and purpose visit him, and pass away, and are forgotten !

And so now, addressing some who may be meditating such a return—and some who, through God's grace, have even realized it—I would suggest a few thoughts to-day with reference to the Home-life on which you are entering ; that life, I mean, which comes after the first turning to God ; that life which ought to continue—which God grant may continue in us—from this time forth till we die and are safe for ever.

The Home-life of the Restored—that is the last part of our subject. Having returned to God— having received His blessed welcome to that spiritual home, of His love and presence, which our sins had forfeited—how shall we retain that blessedness? how shall we keep upon our souls the freshness of that pardon and of that acceptance, so that, when we die, we may be ready for the real home—for the family of the just made perfect?

And here I would say—

First, we must *form our expectations truly.* In

the first days of repentance, while the soul is feeling after God, and just beginning to grasp the promise and to lay hold upon the great Sacrifice which is our hope, there is usually a stir and excitement within, which powerfully affects the whole course and current of our being. Where the work is strong and earnest, there is in the first days a natural expectation that the whole of life will be of this character; that the day will be occupied in communion, and the night in praise. And when this is not found so to be; when the inward life is found to fluctuate like the outward; when hope itself loses its freshness, and the experience of lingering or reviving sin disappoints the calculation of a rapid progress towards perfection; then comes, too often, weariness, languor, depression, despondency; at last, relaxed effort, acquiescence in low attainment, inconsistencies of speech and habit; in the end, amidst many half-recoveries, even a falling away from grace once given, a tarnished and sullied if not forfeited crown. It might not have been thus, if the expectations of the young Christian had been more truly formed.

Expect not—we should say to ourselves—the

permanence of your first feeling. You are entering upon what may prove to be a long life of Christian faith and duty. This life will bring with it, of necessity, many experiences. There will be in it long periods of sameness, monotony, dulness. Duty itself will often look very commonplace, very unimportant, sometimes very unattractive. The spirits will vary with varying health, and even the soul will oftentimes ebb and flow with both. There will often be an impression upon your mind that you are doing little good, that your endeavours find little success, and your prayers no answer. Sometimes, when you have been living for years in the Home of which we speak, you will almost feel, like the Elder Son in the Parable, that a sort of injustice is done to you; that, instead of thanks or reward, you are only suffered and taken (as it were) for granted: for others, the wilful wandering ones, the fatted calf is killed; their recovery is hailed, with transports of joy, as life from the dead: there are no outbreaks of joy over you; your service is treated as a matter of course, eliciting no wonder, and recompensed by no reward.

Frame your expectations beforehand on these

suppositions. Recognize these as the natural experiences of a long Home-life. Think how it is
in an earthly home. It is the stranger son who
makes its excitements. It is the return which
draws forth the welcome. The sister who is always there—bearing its burdens, smoothing its
roughnesses, allaying its little discords—she is not
thanked, she is not praised : yet, if she were to
die, she would be the one missed ! It is somewhat thus in God's family, the household of His
true servants, the community of His spiritual
Church. Be well contented if God should ever
say to you, *Son, thou art ever with me.* That is
higher praise, surer comfort, after all, than the tur-
bulent jubilee which welcomes home the prodigal !
This, too, perhaps, was once yours : wish not that
it should be yours again ! That first welcome,
joyful as it is, is purchased but by long wandering :
be it yours to wander no more ! say rather now,
*This God is my God for ever and ever : He shall be
my Guide unto death !*

And then, having formed our expectations justly,
we must, in the second place, be careful to *live by
the rules of the Home.*

Here again a life of mere feeling is out of place.
We want rules. We require the curb of rule to
keep us orderly, and we require the stimulus of
rule to keep us active. If we are to wait for the
prompting of inclination, to pray, to read, to meditate, to worship, to commune, to communicate,
we shall wait long and wait in vain. We must set
ourselves, in the very outset of a home-life with
God, to live by the home-rules. No earthly household could prosper, in which the caprice or the
appetite of each inmate was to be the prescriber
of its hours of food and resting : so is it with
God's House. In the first moments and days of a
great conversion, there will be eagerness enough
for opportunities of grace : but that life thrives
best, in the long run, which is lived by rule ; that
life, which has its fixed times of waiting upon
God, and resolutely keeps to them, year after year,
without waiting for inward impulses of strong inclination or conscious imperious need. The Home-
life of the Restored must be marked by a rigid
conscientious adherence to the rules of the Household. We must take our place in it as sons ;
thankfully adapting ourselves to its Master's

wishes, and, whether at the moment we will or no, carefully doing the thing which He says.

There is a third thing. He who would live the Home-life of the Restored, and be found in it when the Master comes, must *throw himself thoroughly into the life.* Sometimes in earthly homes a son or a daughter lodges within the house, who is in reality no part of the household; so entirely distinct from it are the real interests, so completely elsewhere the friendships and the affections. Such an inmate is an incubus upon the home. There is no help there for the rest, because there is no sympathy and no incorporation. Alas! how true a picture of that which many Christians are in God's Home! If we would ever live the restored life—live it so as to belong to it, live it so as to be a part of it—we must throw all our sympathies, all our interests, all our hearts into it. Let its society be your society, its work your work, its honour your joy, its defeat your sorrow! It is here that we fail. Willing to enjoy the privilege of Christian worship, hoping to enter into the Christian rest, we are not, heart and soul, inside the family, *bound up* (as

Scripture says) *in the bundle of life with it,* having
it for the business of busy days, and for the rising
and resting meditation of calm silent nights, how
we may further its aims and help its triumphs.
He will never be safe in God's house who sits
loose to it : he who would abide in it for ever
must see that his heart be there. God give us
this, and all shall be well !

Lastly, we would say, *Look on far enough.* Fix
your thoughts on the end. Let no impatience
rob you of the real blessedness—to be *found of
Him in peace.* In the happiness of the home—
even of God's home—below, forget not the great
return, forget not the great welcome ! More or
less, we are wanderers still, the best of us : without
leaving the home, we can err and stray within it :
we have still to say, in some sense, *I will arise and
go to my Father:* and not until death comes, or the
Advent, can that purpose be absolutely fulfilled.
See that we miss it not ! Let us so use God's
Home on earth ; the means of grace, the ordinances of prayer and praise and communion, the
opportunity of ministering to Christ in His poor
and in His children, the blessed power, given to

each of us, of making some little return for all the benefits that He has done to us, at least by *receiving the cup of salvation and calling upon the name of the Lord;* that at last we may hear the glad welcome into a heavenly home, *Come, ye blessed of my Father—enter thou into the joy of thy Lord!*

Ballantyne and Company, Printers, Edinburgh.

www.ingramcontent.com/pod-product-compliance
Lightning Source LLC
Chambersburg PA
CBHW060513030726
47498CB00004B/927